BADLANDS
IMPRESSIONS

photography by CHUCK HANEY

text by Dick Kettlewell

FARCOUNTRY PRESS

Right: A soft light spreads across these Cedar Pass formations in South Dakota's Badlands National Park. Established as a national monument in 1939, this preserve was designated as a national park in 1978 and receives more than a million visitors a year.

Title page: Amid early morning fog, the Little Missouri River winds its way through the Little Missouri National Grassland of North Dakota. Covering over one million acres of the state's western half, the Little Missouri is the nation's largest grassland and features the beautiful and colorful badlands of Theodore Roosevelt National Park.

Front cover: Sunrise light breaks through on these lovely sculpted buttes near the Badlands Loop Road in Badlands National Park. This park comprises 242,756 acres of sharply eroded buttes, pinnacles and spires like these that were formed in layers of tiny grains of sediments such as sand, silt and clay cemented together into sedimentary rocks.

Back cover: A passing afternoon thunderstorm brightens the Painted Canyon badlands of North Dakota's Theodore Roosevelt National Park. Established as the Theodore Roosevelt National Memorial Park in 1947 by President Harry Truman, it was the only national memorial park ever nominated as such. In 1978, along with several boundary adjustments, the park's designation was changed to Theodore Roosevelt National Park.

ISBN: 978-1-56037-579-1

Text by Dick Kettlewell

For more information about our books, write Farcountry Press, P.O. Box 5630, Helena, MT 59604; call (800) 821-3874; or visit www.farcountrypress.com.

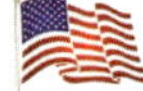
Produced and printed in the United States of America.

26 25 24 23 22   2 3 4 5 6

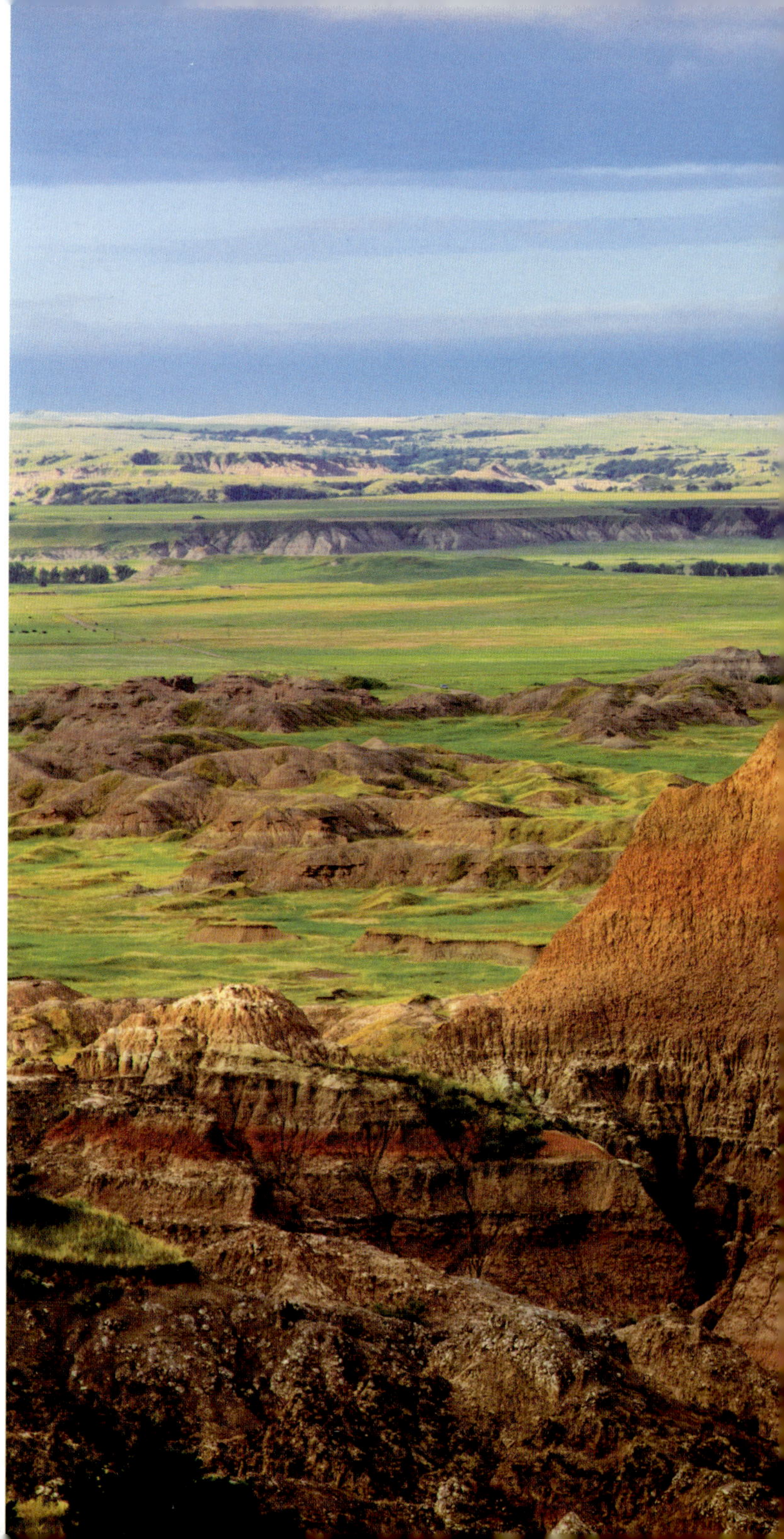

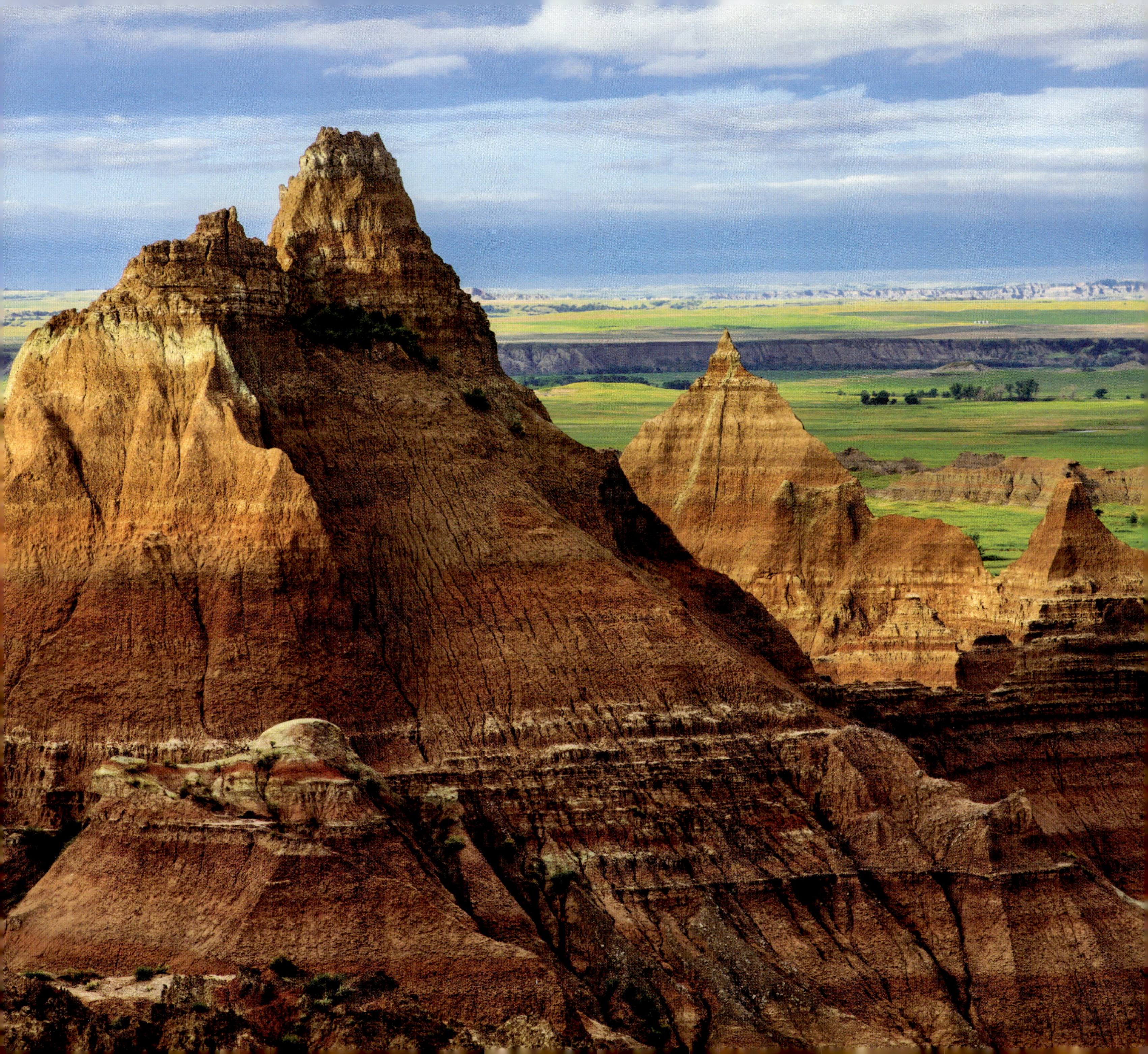

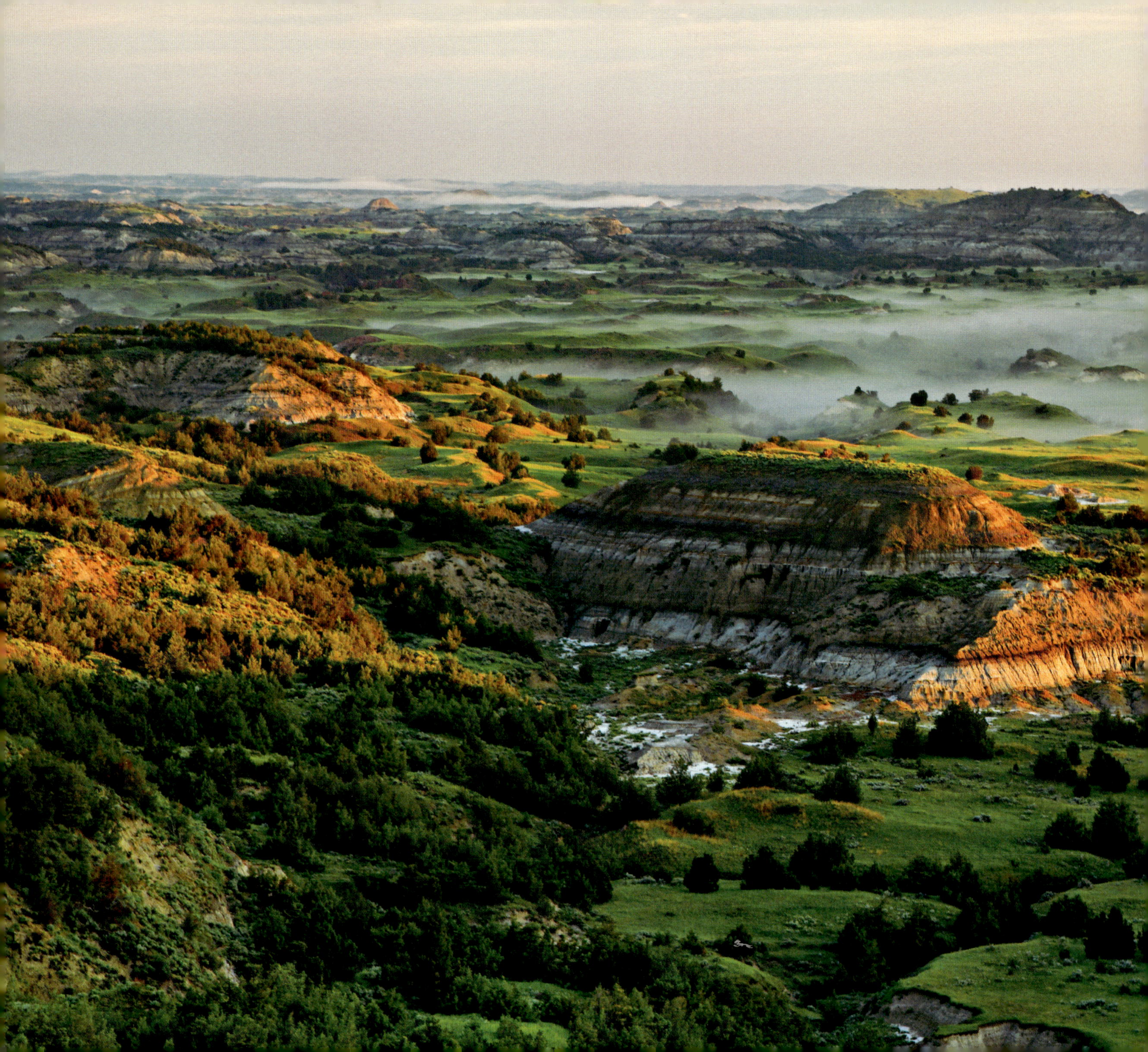

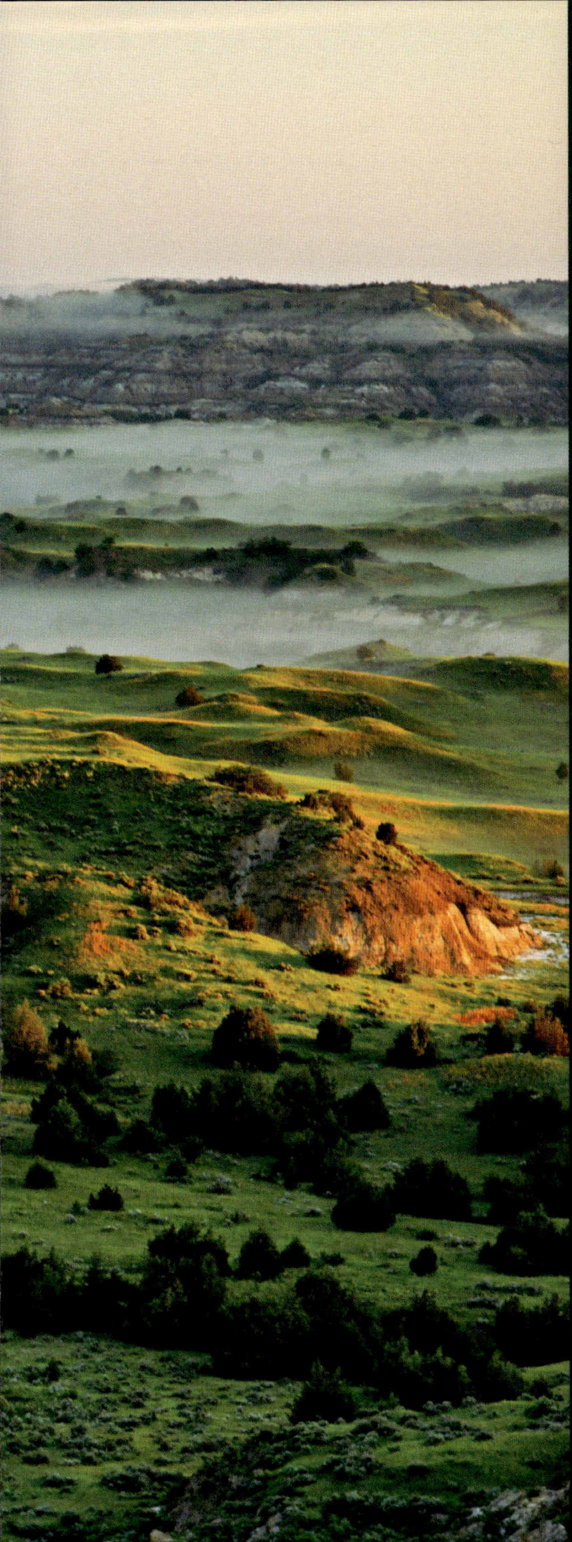

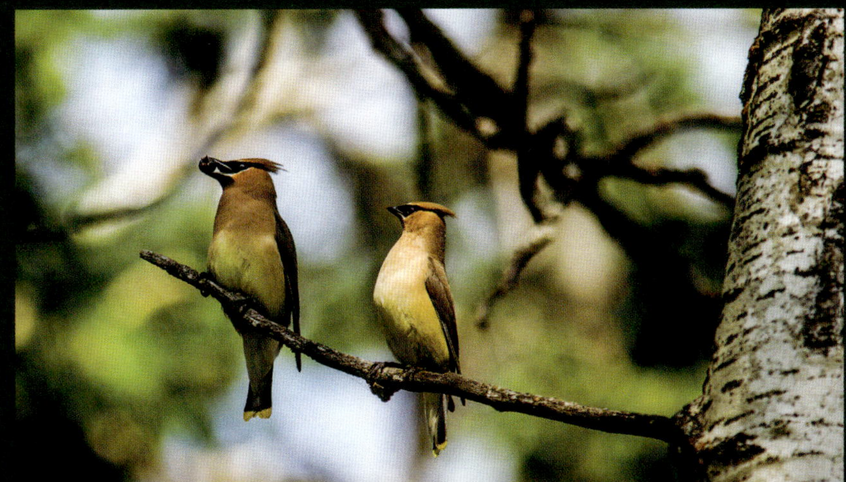

Above: A pair of cedar waxwings *(Bombycilla cedrorum)* perch on the small branch of a birch tree in North Dakota's Lake Metigoshe State Park. The cedar waxwing is a medium-sized bird that is native to North and Central America, feeding on a diet of berries and insects. This park is located on the shores of Lake Metigoshe along the Canada-US border.

Left: Morning fog moves across the badlands of Theodore Roosevelt National Park, bringing a chill to the day's beginning. This park comprises three geographically separate areas of badlands in western North Dakota and covers 70,446 acres. It is the nation's only national park named for a person.

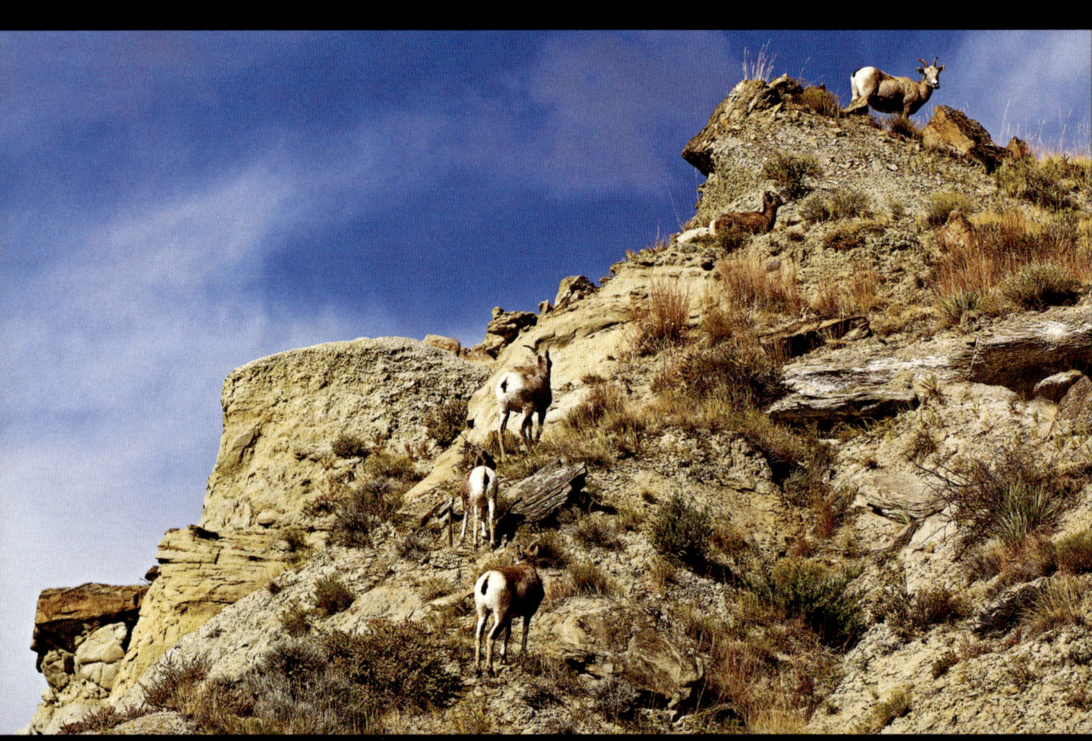

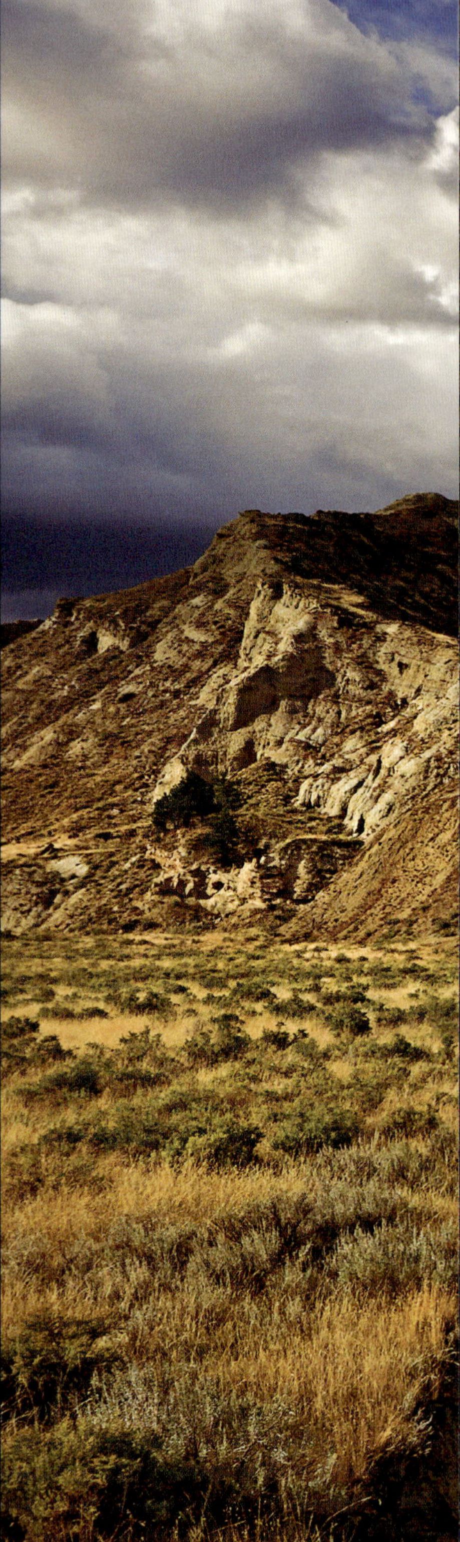

Above: Bighorn sheep *(Ovis canadensis)* make their way up a set of cliffs at the Upper Missouri River Breaks National Monument in Montana. The Lewis and Clark Expedition passed through this area in 1805, becoming the first white explorers to sight and document bighorn sheep. This country was a model for the prolific painter and illustrator of the American West, Charles M. Russell.

Right: Under a cloud-filled sky, a caprock formation rises above the landscape near Little Bullwhacker Creek in Upper Missouri River Breaks National Monument. In 1877, Chief Joseph along with his Nez Perce warriors crossed the Missouri River nearby during their attempted escape to Canada from the U.S. Army. This action led to a brief skirmish at Cow Island Landing.

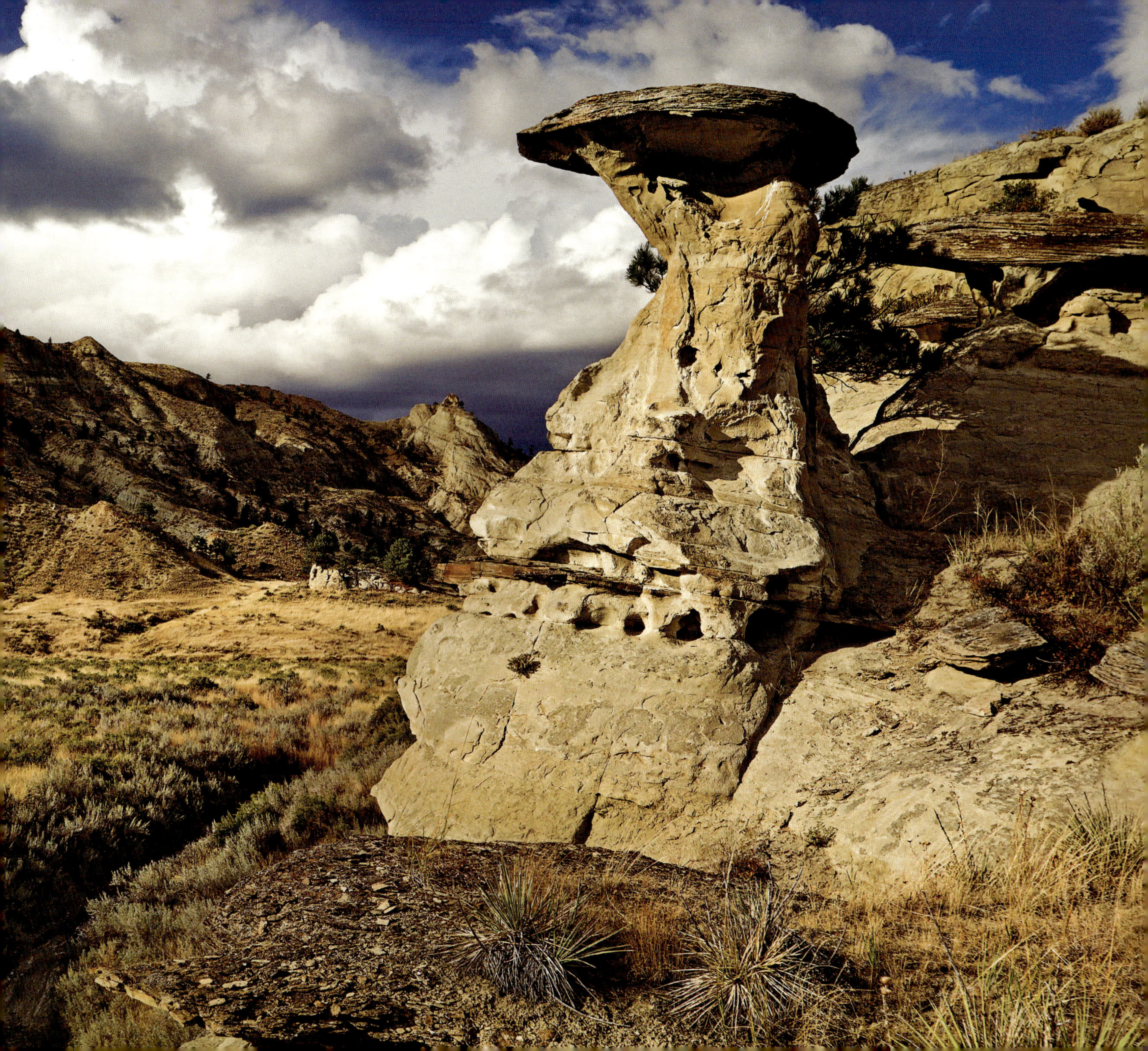

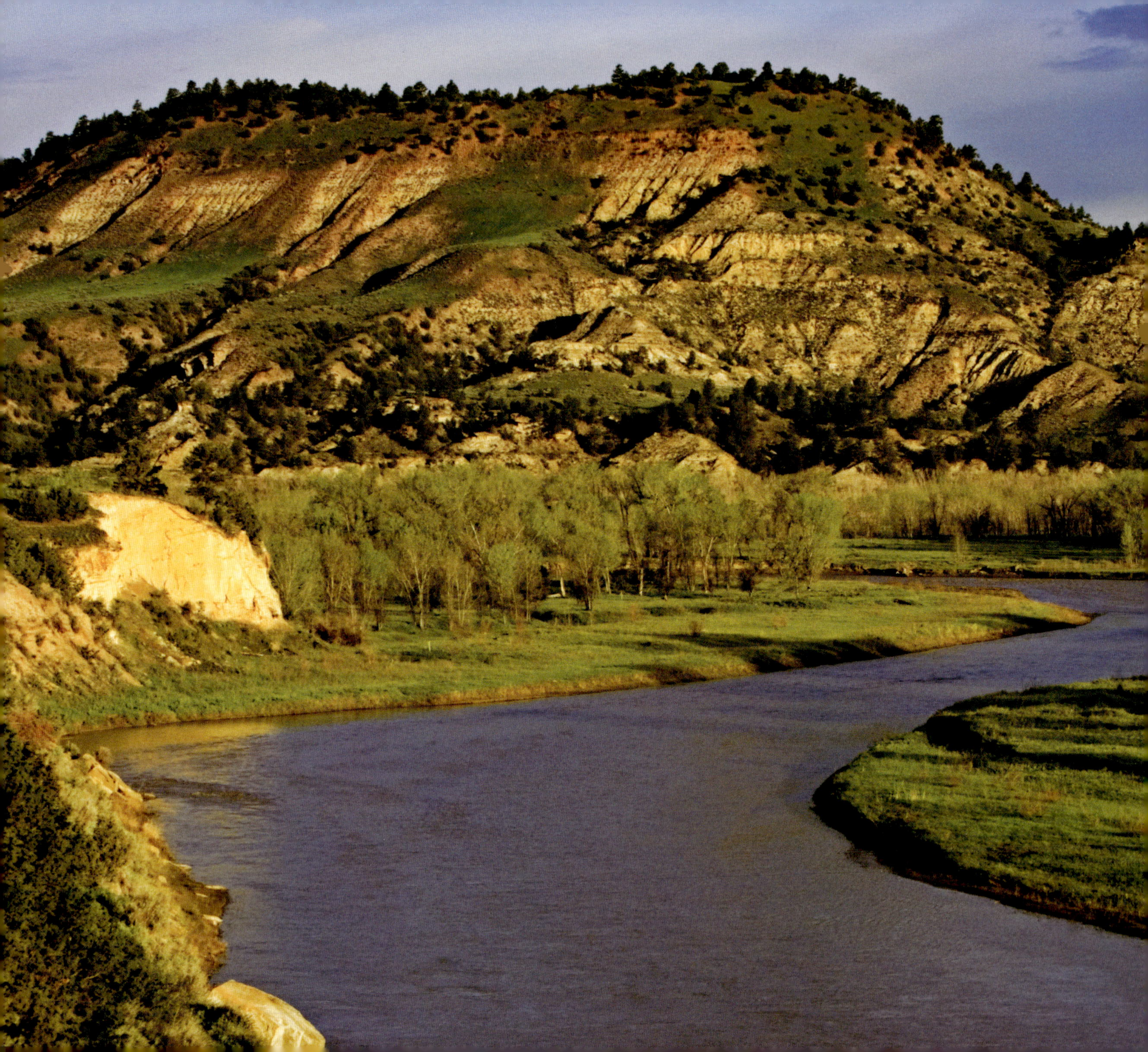

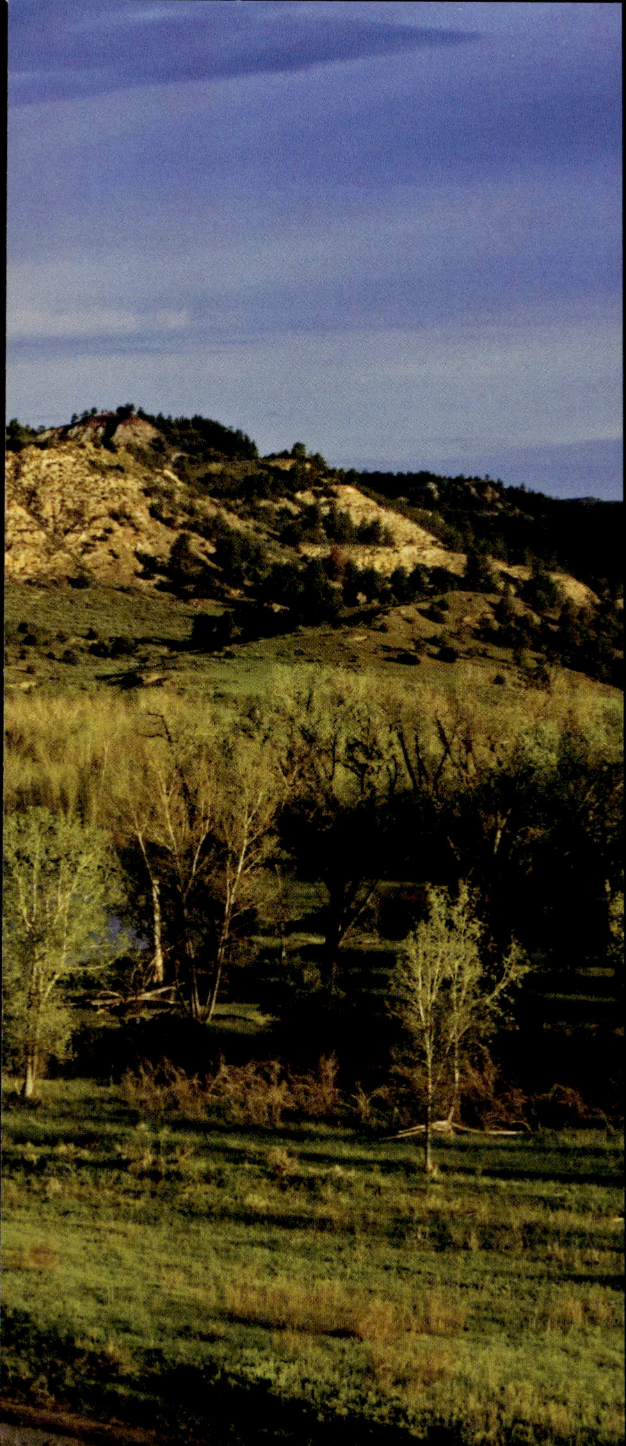

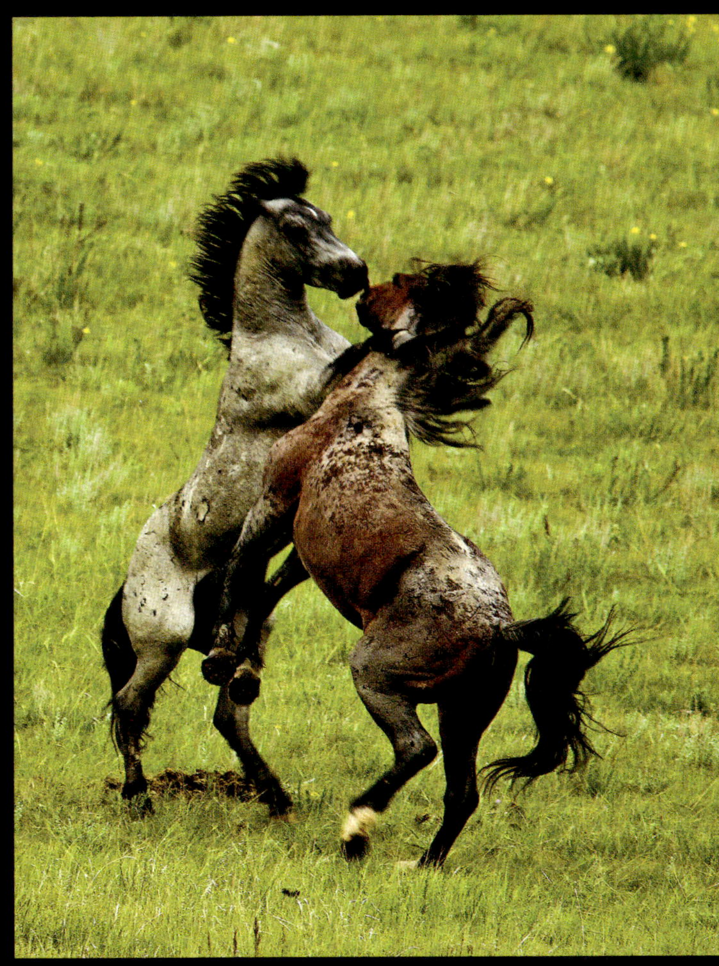

Above: Two wild horses *(Equus ferus)* roughhouse in one of the grassland meadows of Theodore Roosevelt National Park. These animals are actually "feral," meaning they are wild descendants of domesticated animals. Feral horses have existed on the badlands of western North Dakota since the mid-1800s.

Left: The Powder River winds lazily past bluffs accented by cliffs and scattered forests near Broadus, Montana. This river, approximately 375 miles long, is a tributary of the Yellowstone River and runs from northeastern Wyoming to southeastern Montana. The Powder River was so named because the sand along a portion of its banks resembles powder or dust.

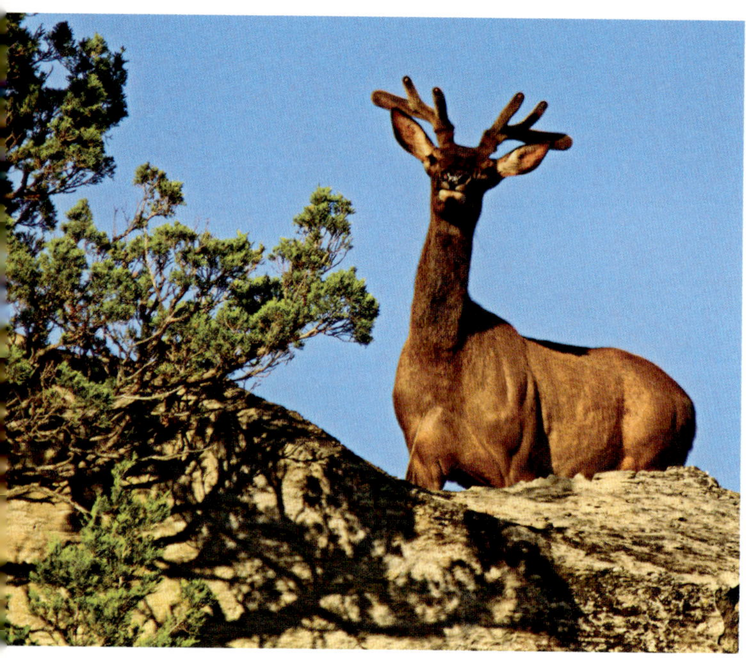

Above: A young bull elk *(Cervus elaphus)* in velvet casts a wary eye across the badlands landscape. This rugged terrian is home to an immense variety of wildlife that includes bison, cougars, coyotes, feral horses, badgers, bighorn sheep, prairie dogs, white-tailed deer, and mule deer.

Right: Sunrise burns off the fog that has gathered above the River Bend Overlook in the North Unit of Theodore Roosevelt National Park. The park's three geographically separate sections include the North Unit, the South Unit, and the Elkhorn Ranch Unit, with the Maah Daah Hey Trail connecting all three units.

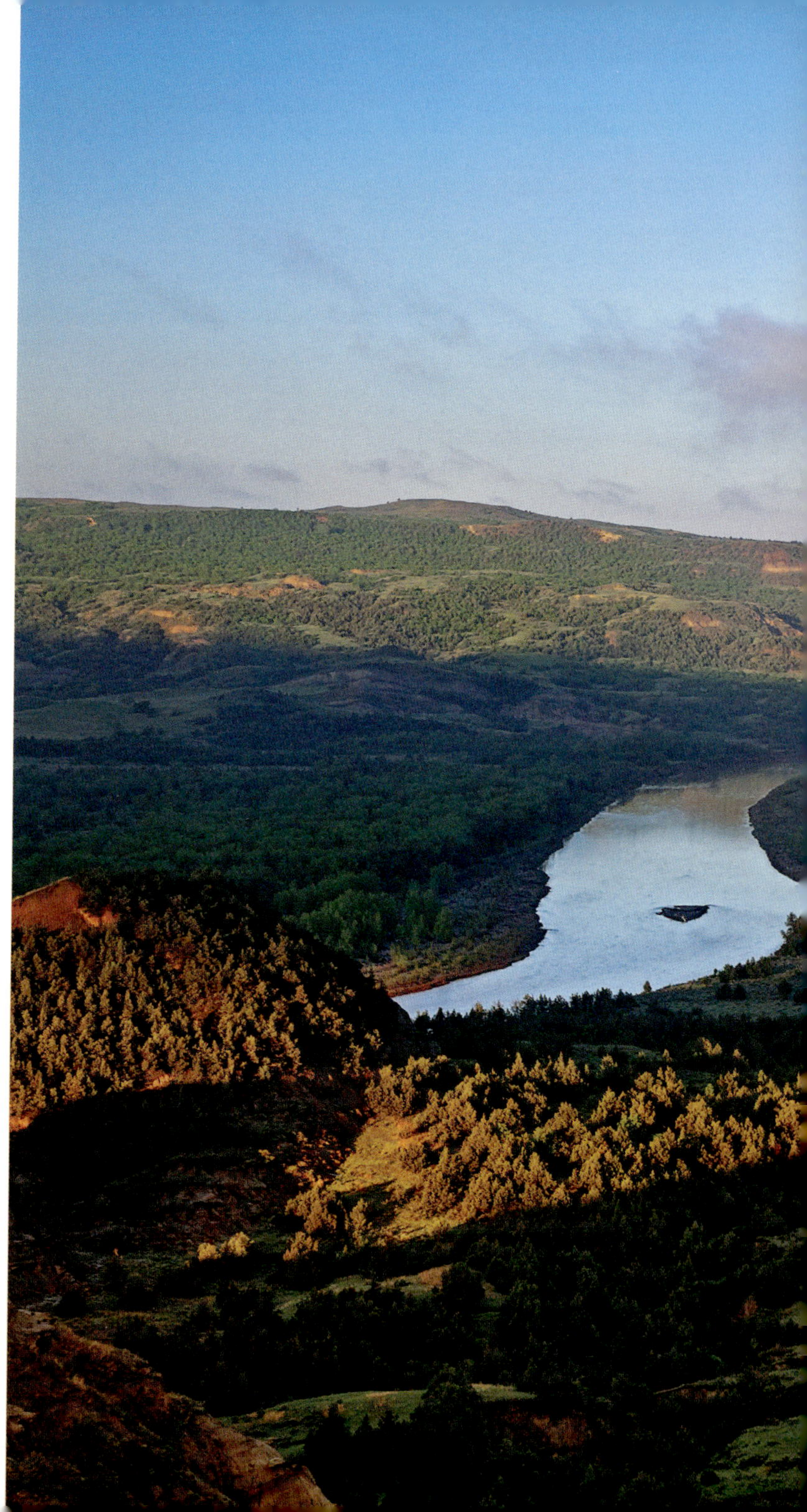

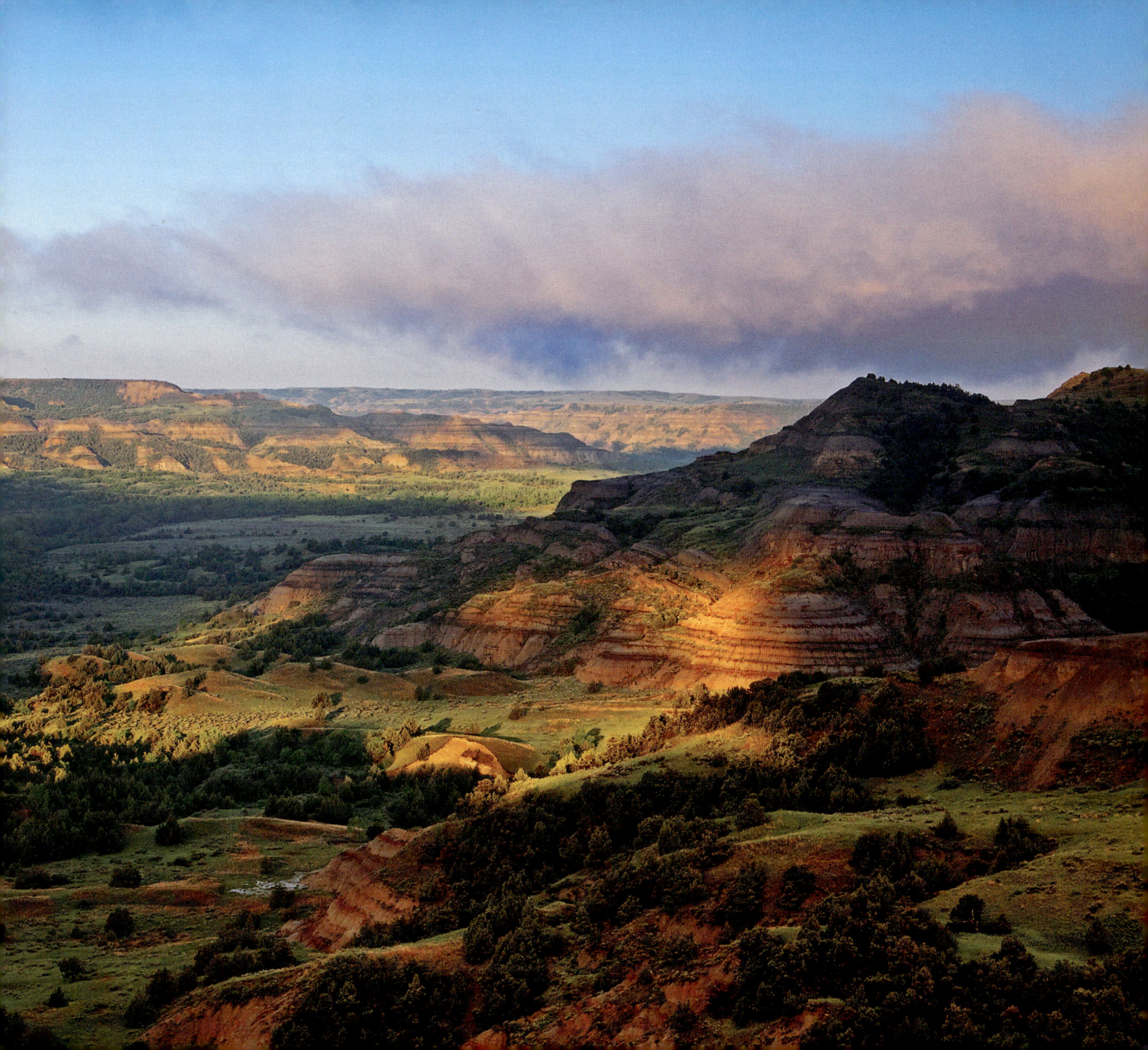

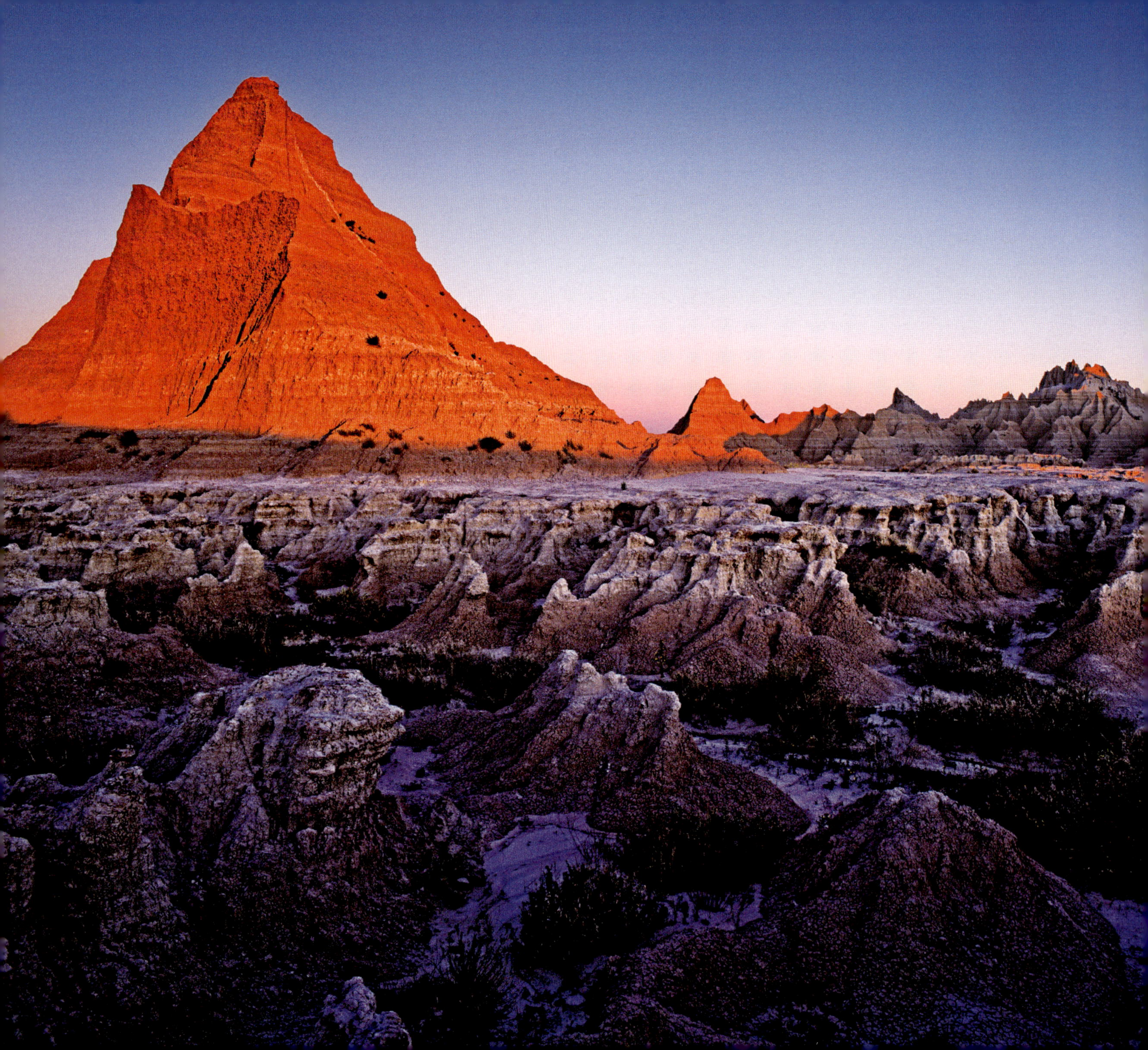

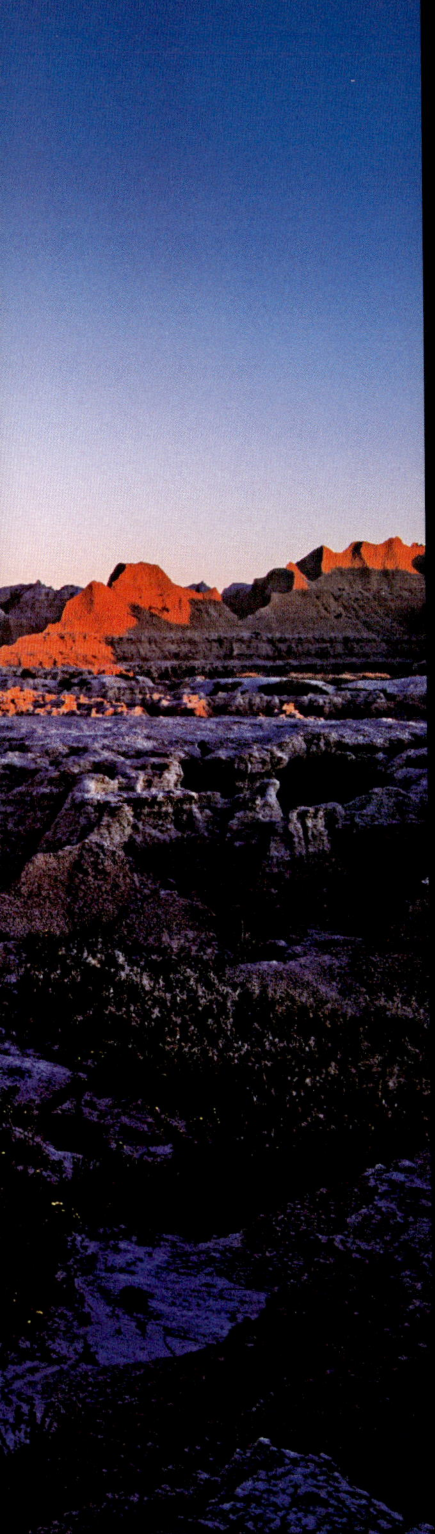

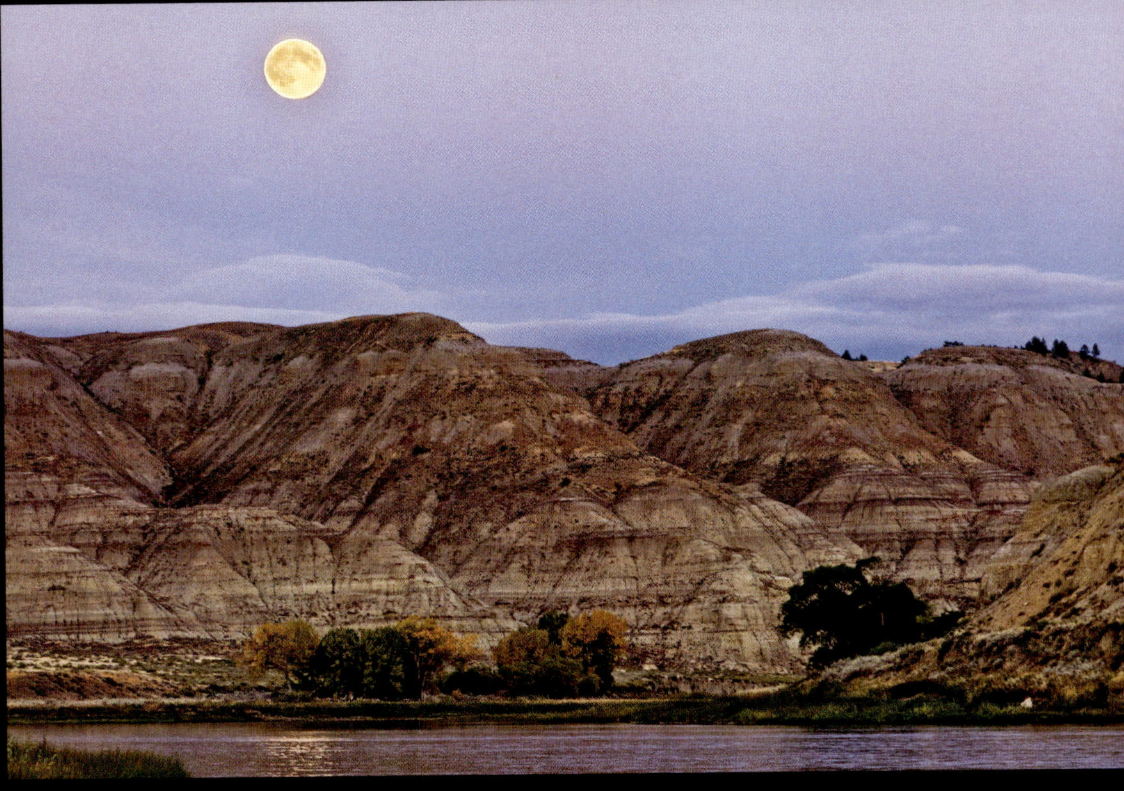

Above: A full moon rises over the badlands of the Upper Missouri River Breaks National Monument as it is reflected in the river's meandering waters, a perfect combination twilight and moonglow.

Left: Badlands National Park is rich in geological preservation and history. Formations like these were formed over three different geologic periods that saw the rise and decline of radically different environments—sea, tropical land, and open woodlands with meandering rivers. The oldest formations are at the bottom with the youngest near the top.

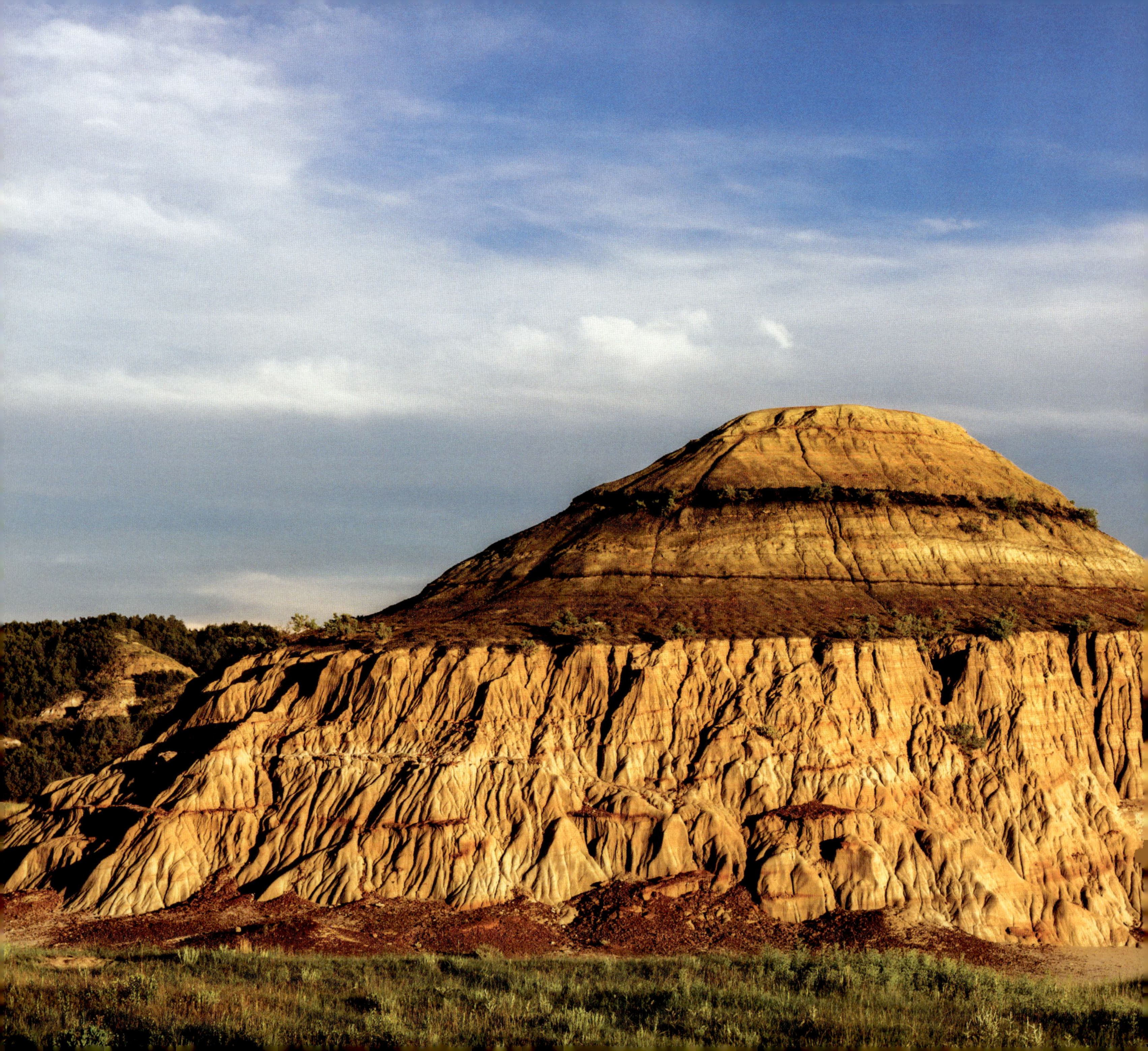

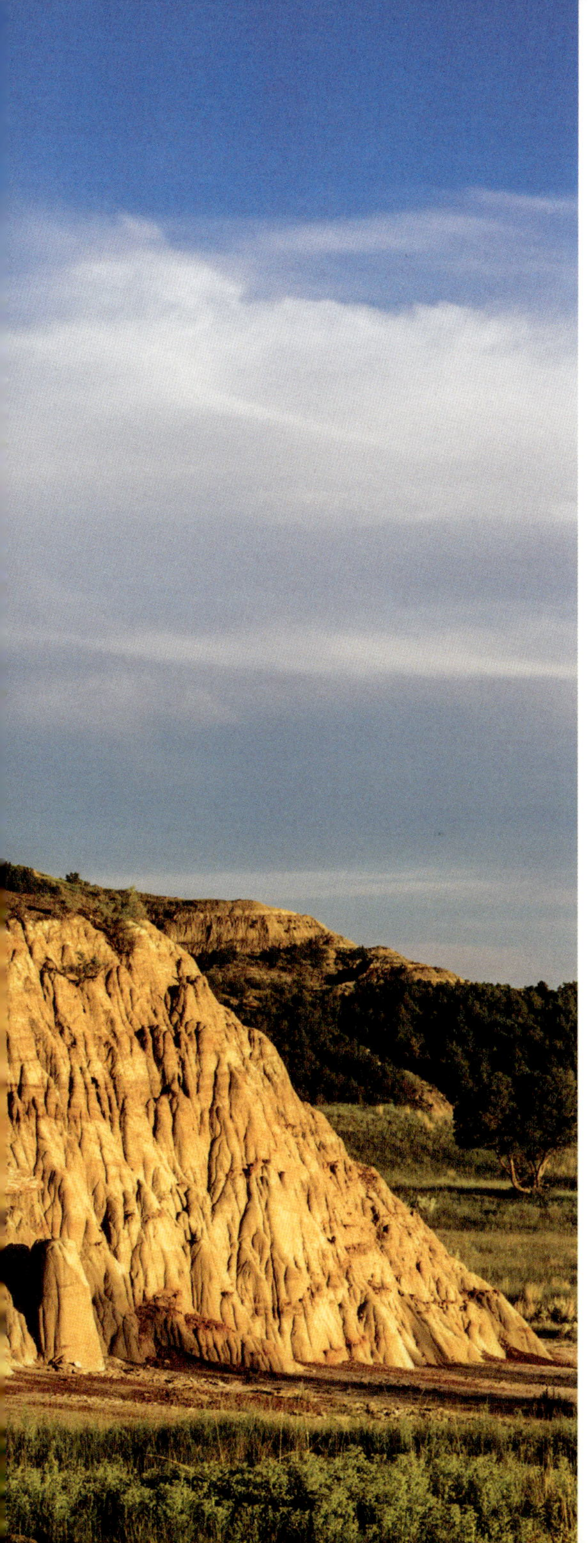

Left: This huge butte makes up part of the badlands that are the dominant landscape characteristic of Theodore Roosevelt National Park. Badlands are a type of dry terrain in which softer sedimentary rocks and clay-rich soils have undergone extensive erosion by wind and water. Common traits include steep slopes, minimal vegetation, canyons, ravines, gullies, buttes, mesas, and hoodoos.

Below: The Keyhole at Monument Rocks, also known as the Chalk Pyramids, is a popular feature at one of the most unique landscapes of western Kansas. These chalk formations, which include buttes and arches, reach a height of up to 70 feet and were formed about 80 million years ago.

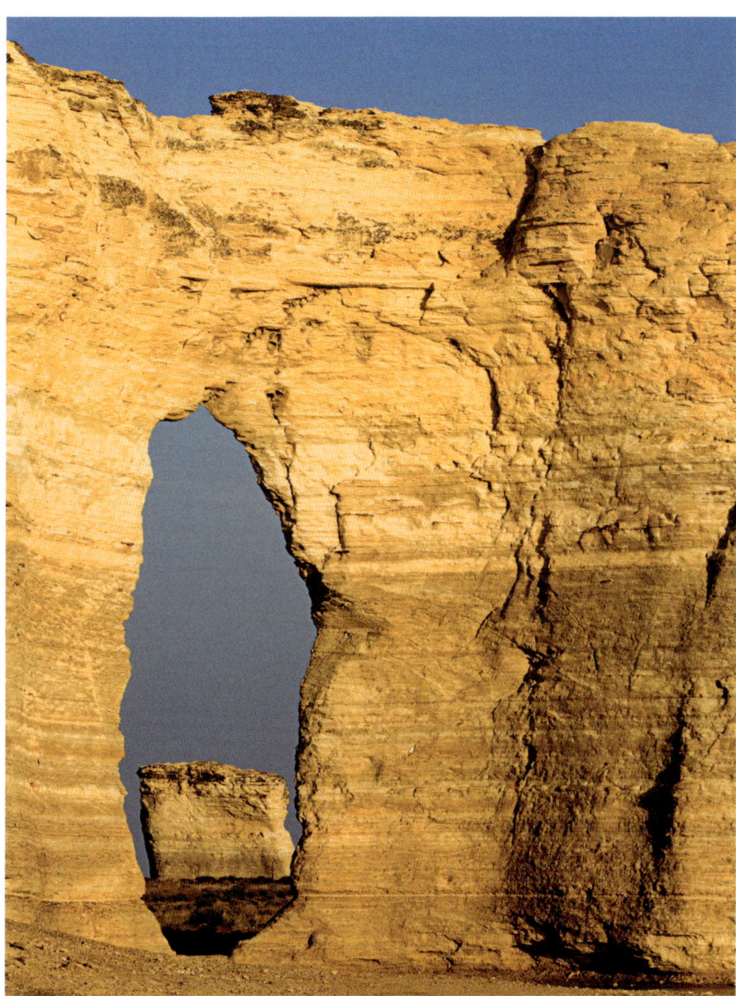

Right: Capitol Rock is a prominent landmark in the Long Pine Hills of Montana's Custer National Forest near the South Dakota border. This forest includes eastern areas dominated by large stands of ponderosa pine and western areas with a mixture of pine, spruce, and fir.

Below: The badlands of western Kansas are lit once again as a thunderstorm passes during late afternoon. This region is prime tornado country with the types of storms that transported Dorothy and her dog in the famous story *The Wizard of Oz.*

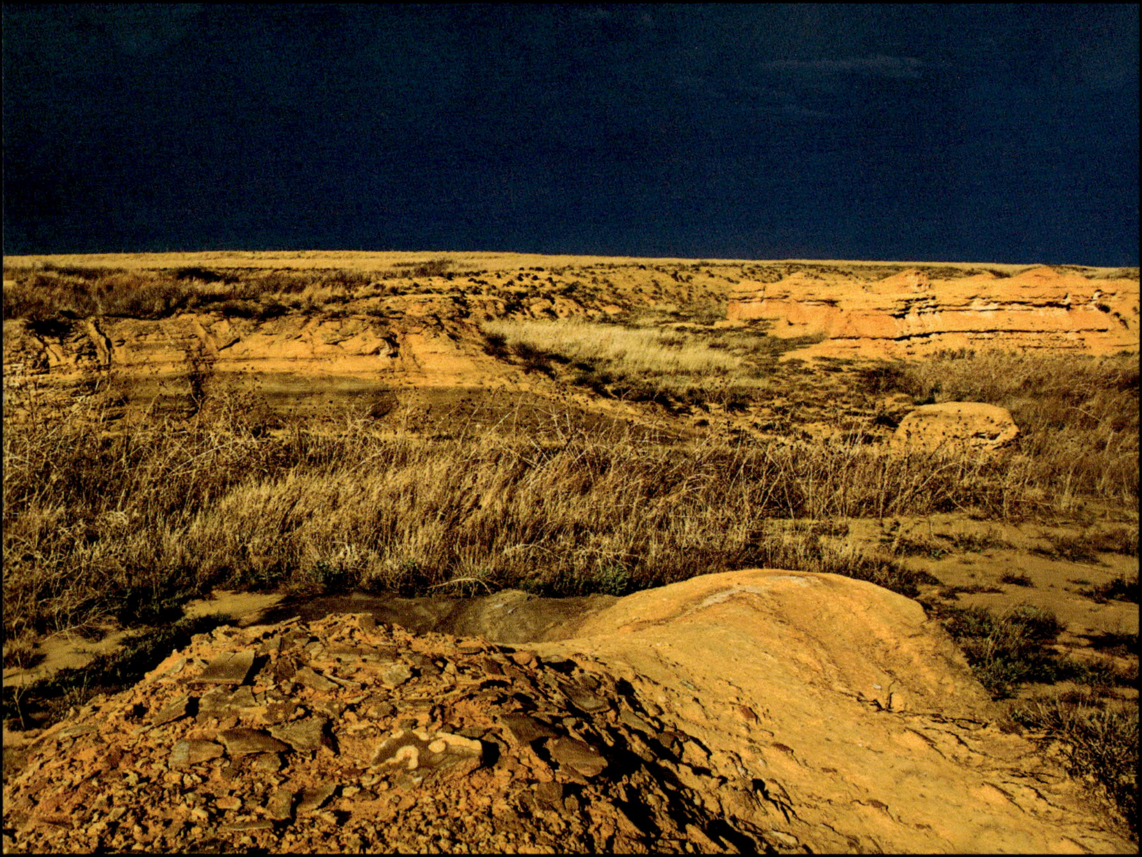

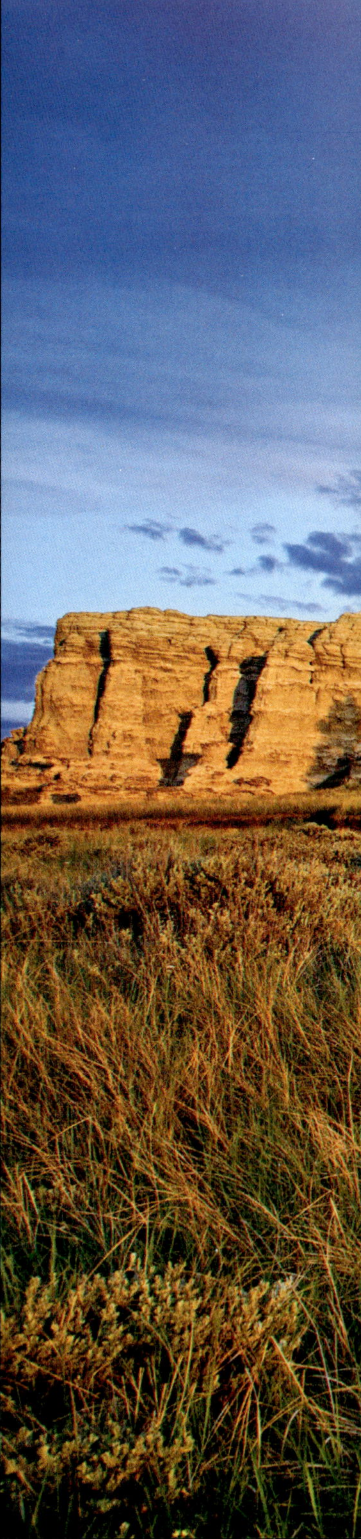

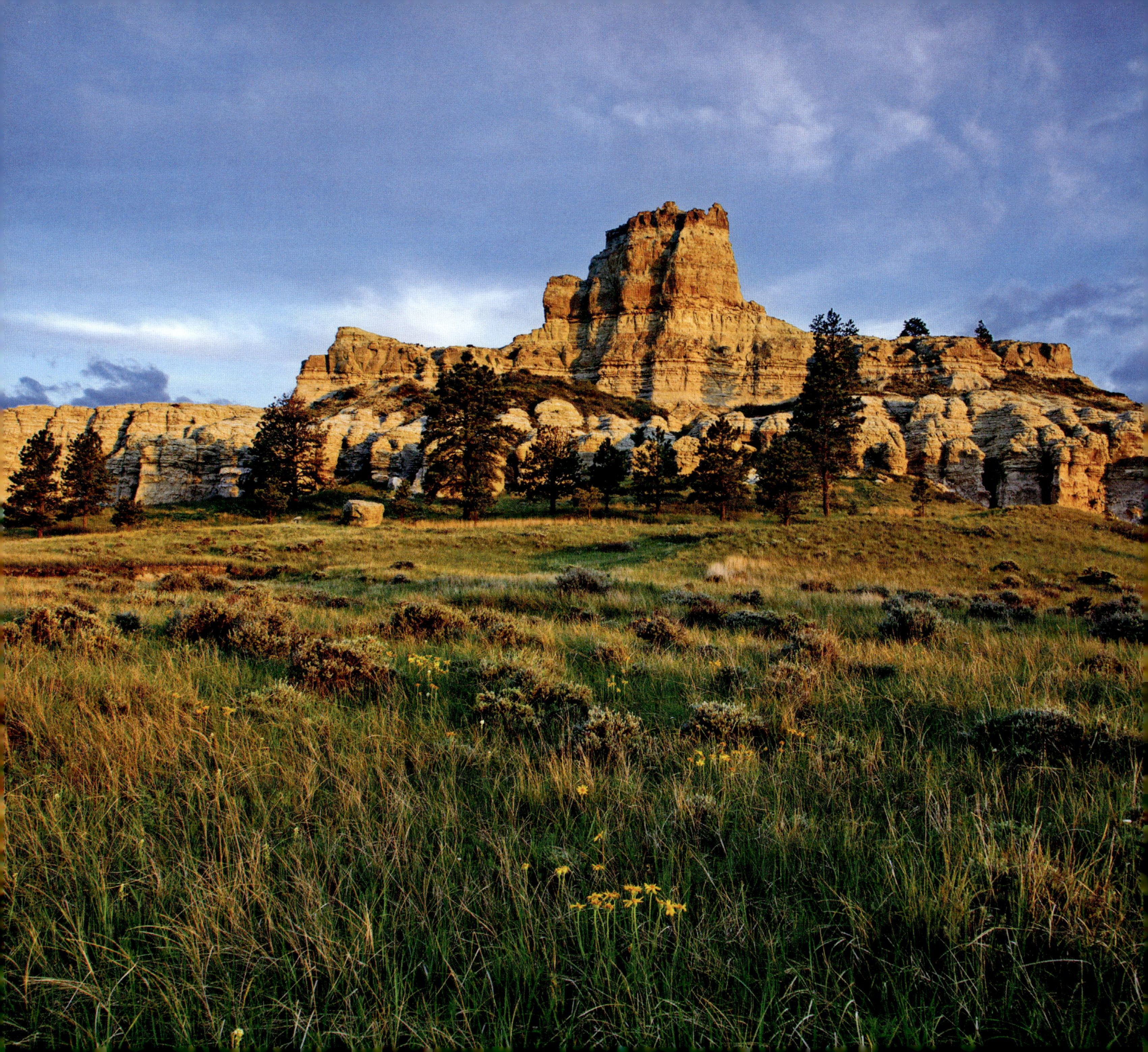

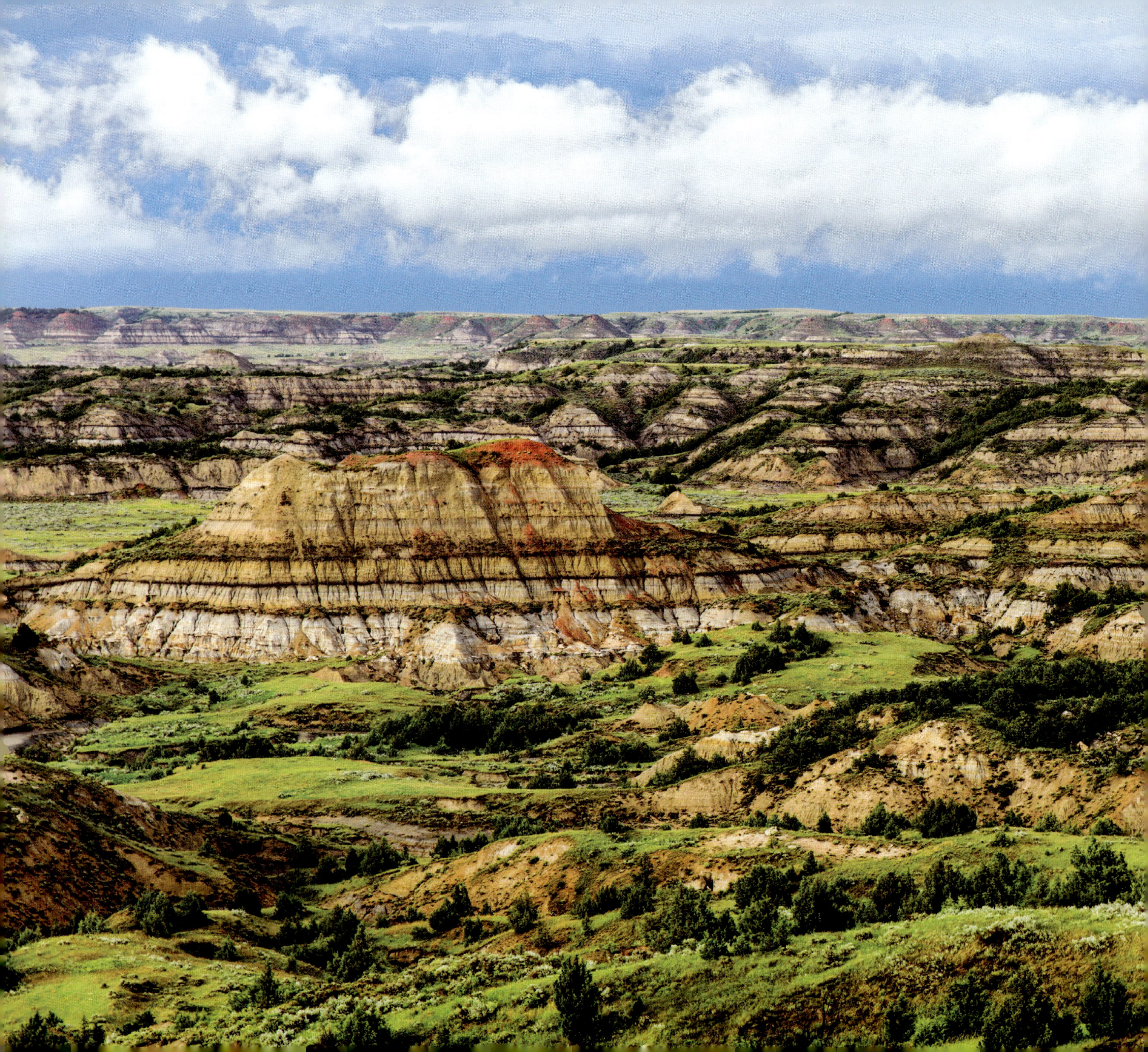

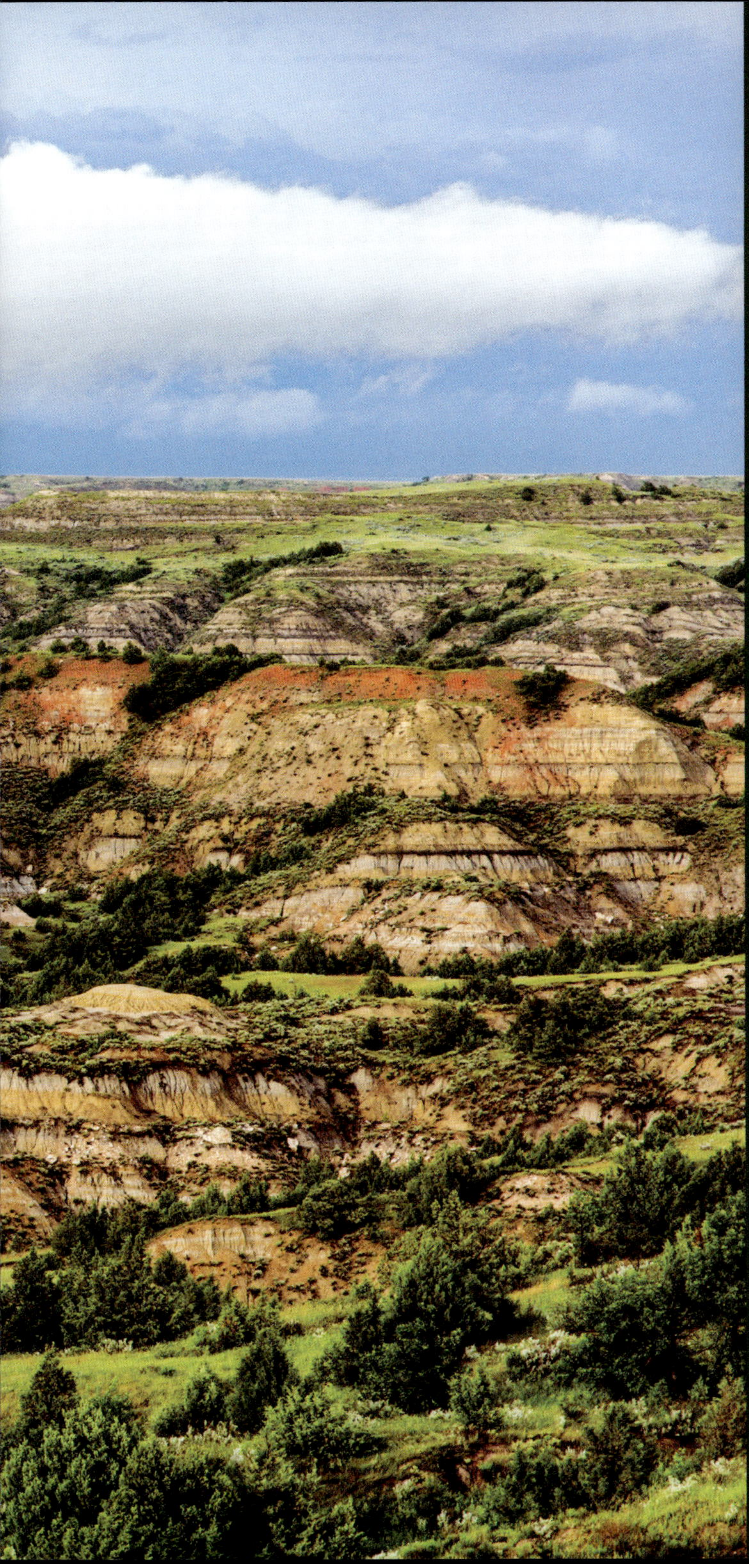

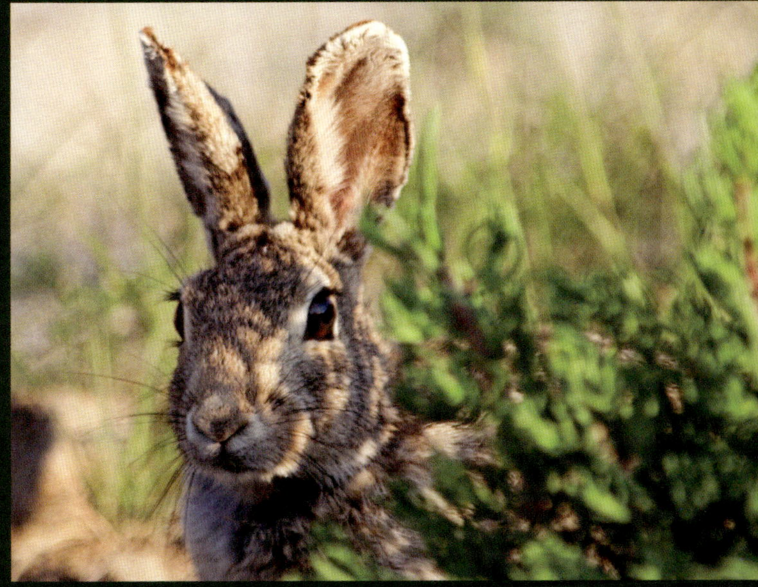

Above: This eastern cottontail rabbit *(Sylvilagus floridanus)* is a prolific breeder, mating as frequently as four times a year and producing four to seven young each time. Exclusively vegetarian, its diet includes bark, twigs, leaves, fruit, buds, flowers, grass seeds, sedge fruits, and rush seeds.

Left: Theodore Roosevelt National Park is especially well known for the colorful badlands of the Painted Canyon and the Maltese Cross Cabin where President Teddy Roosevelt once lived. Roosevelt first came to the North Dakota badlands to hunt bison in September 1883. He returned several months later seeking solace and solitude after the deaths of both his wife and mother on February 14, 1884.

Right: Dense shrubs and thickets are the typical habitat for this gray catbird *(Dumetella carolinensis)*, which is true to its name with a call that sounds like a mewing cat. They generally forage on the ground and in vegetation for a wide variety of insects and berries.

Far right: Blue vervain wildflowers, or woolly verbena *(Verbena stricta)*, fill the grasslands surrounding Red Cloud Buttes at Nebraska's Fort Robinson State Park. Fort Robinson was an important U.S. Army outpost during the Plains Indian wars of the 1870s. The great Lakota war chief Crazy Horse died there in 1877 during an attempted escape from the post guardhouse.

Below: Blue penstemon *(Penstemon angustifoluis)* wildflowers spread down into this ravine in Badlands National Park. Native to the western plains, this perennial generally blooms during May and June.

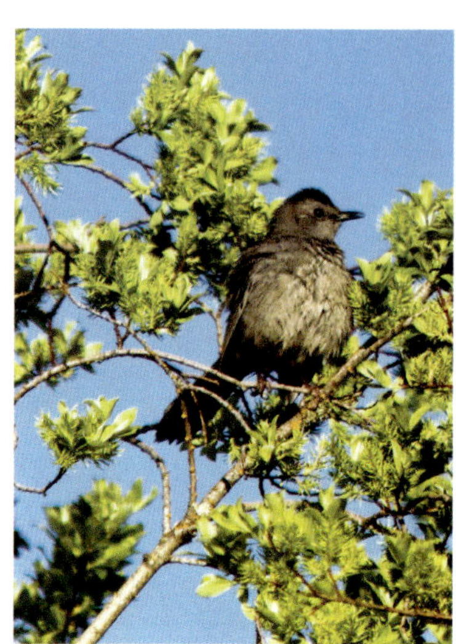

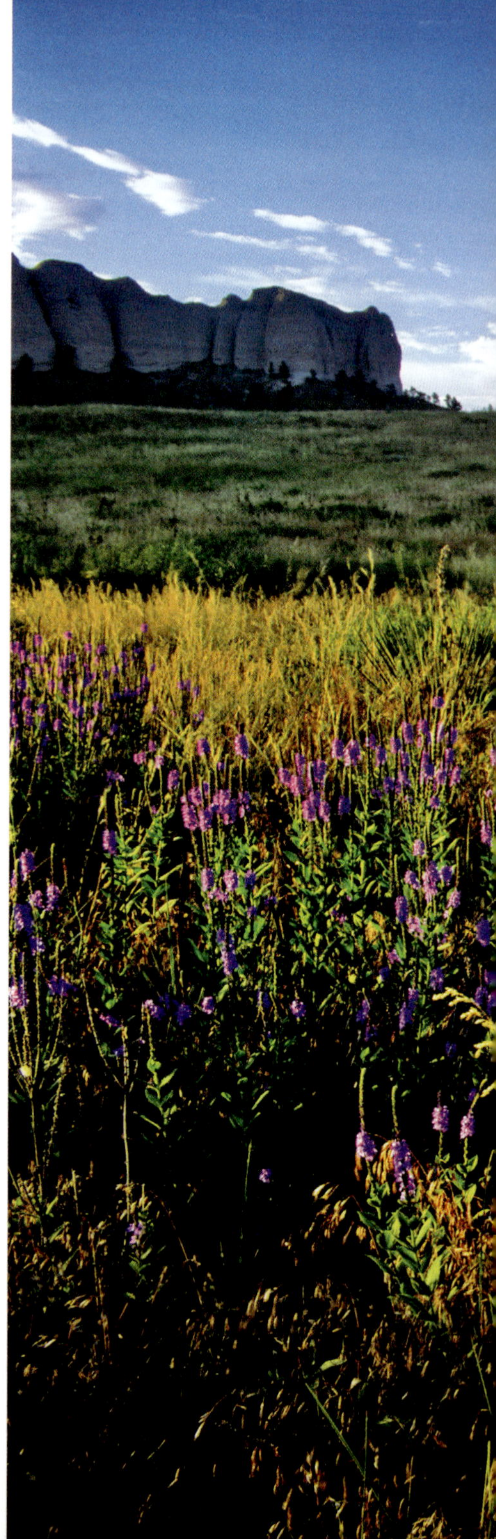

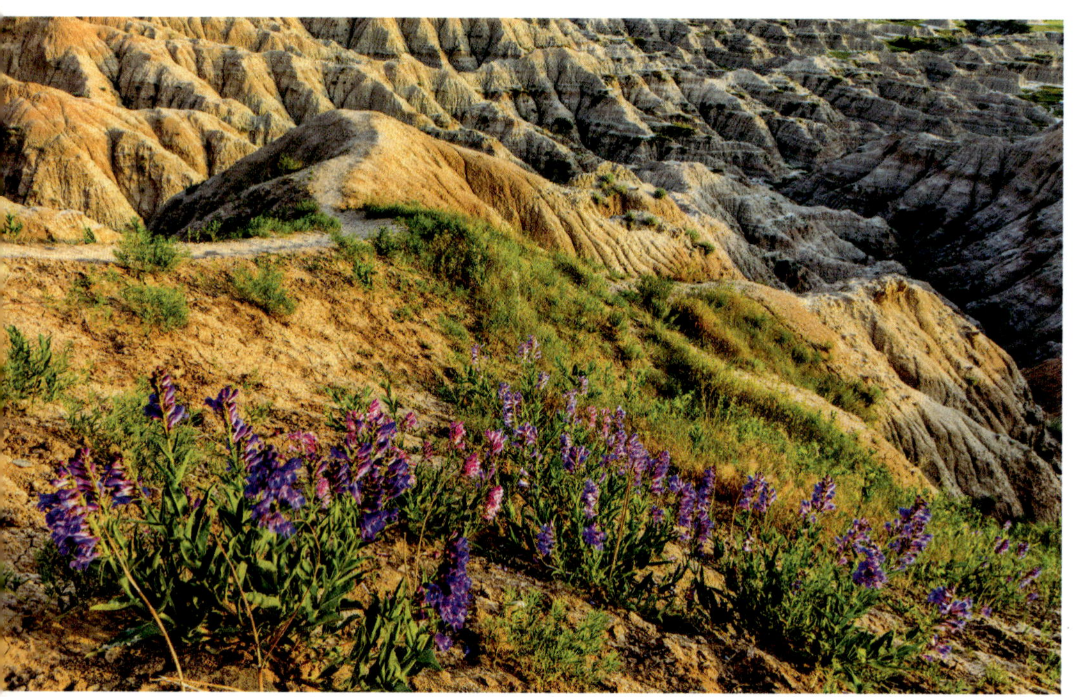

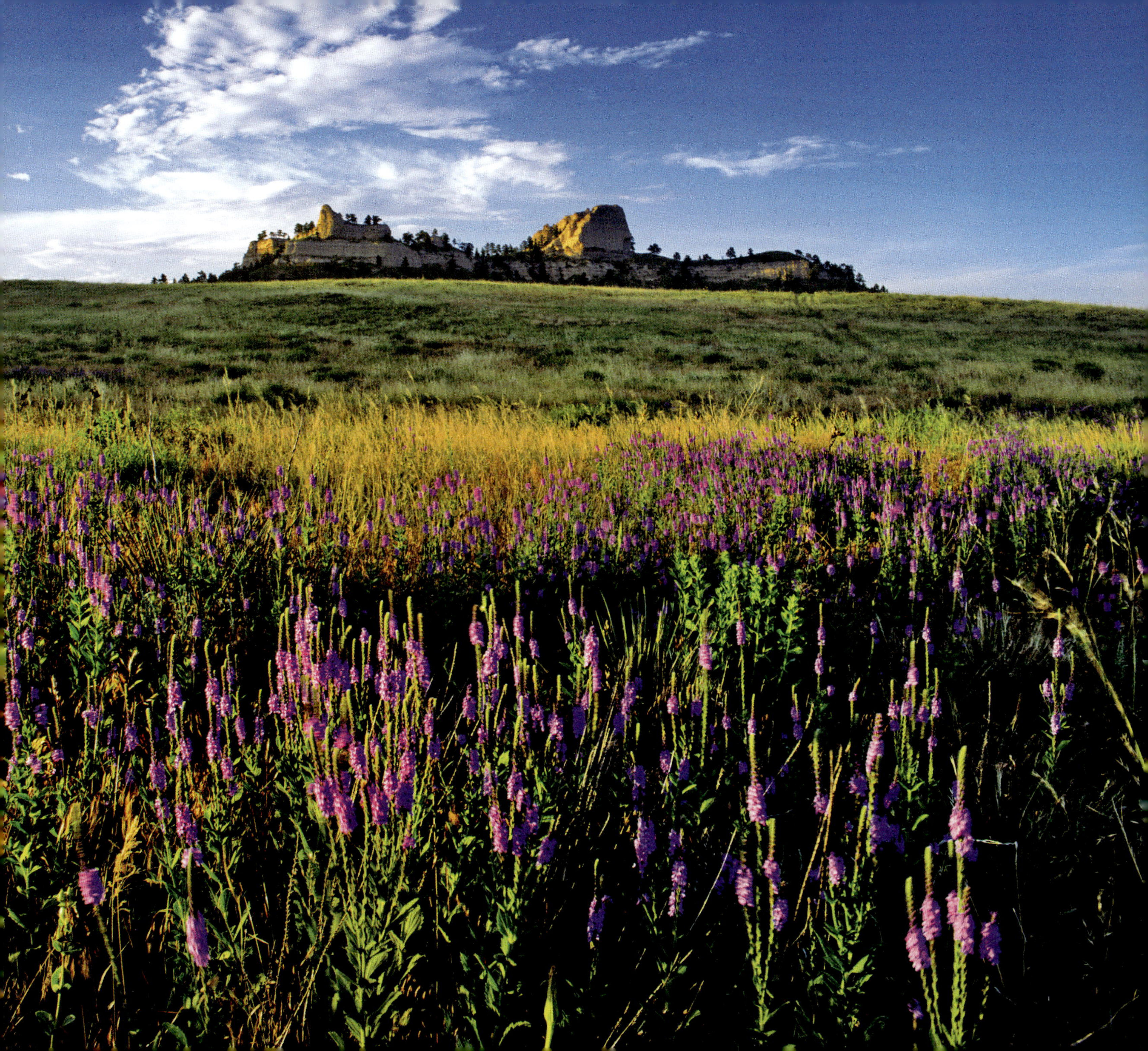

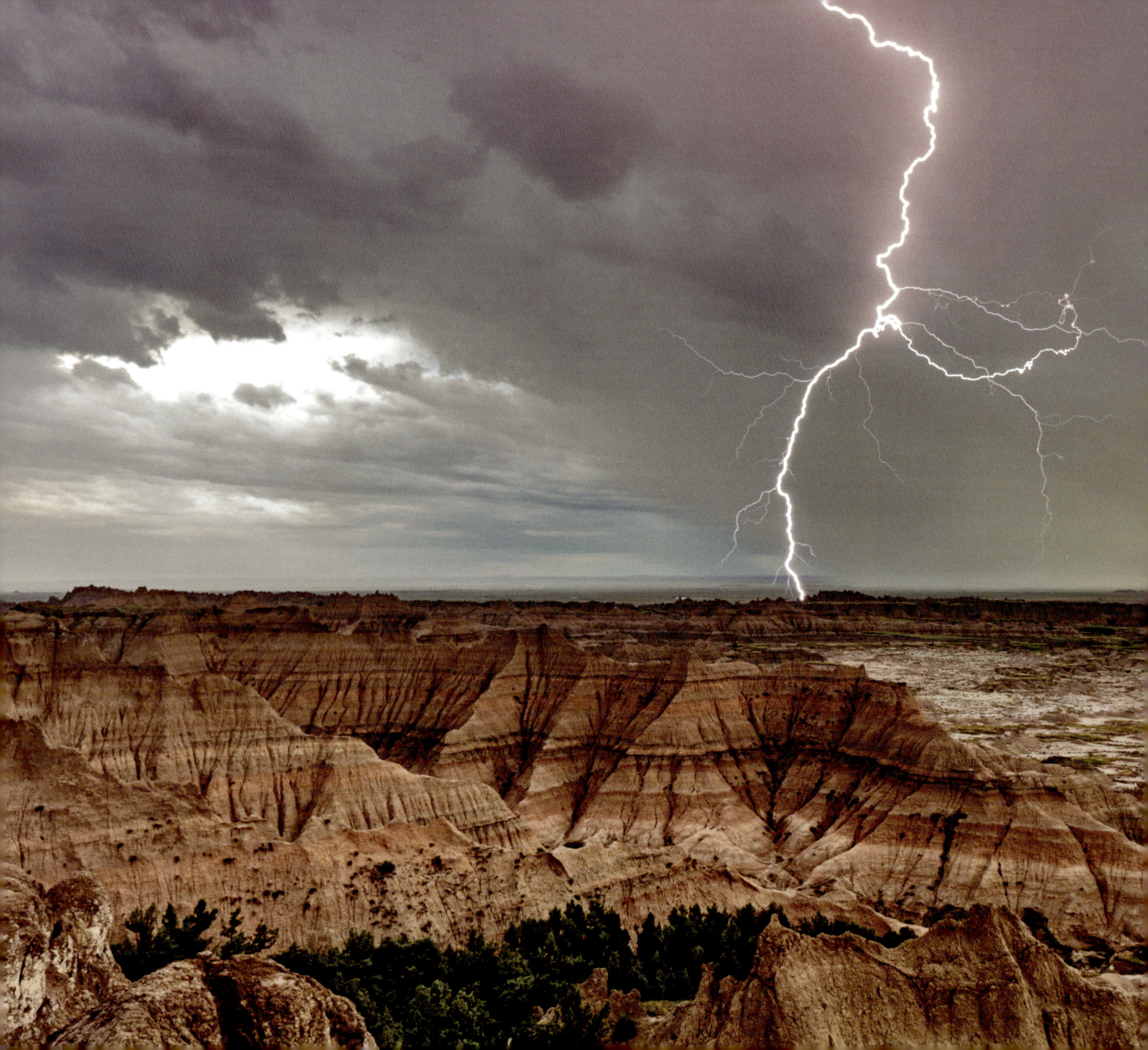

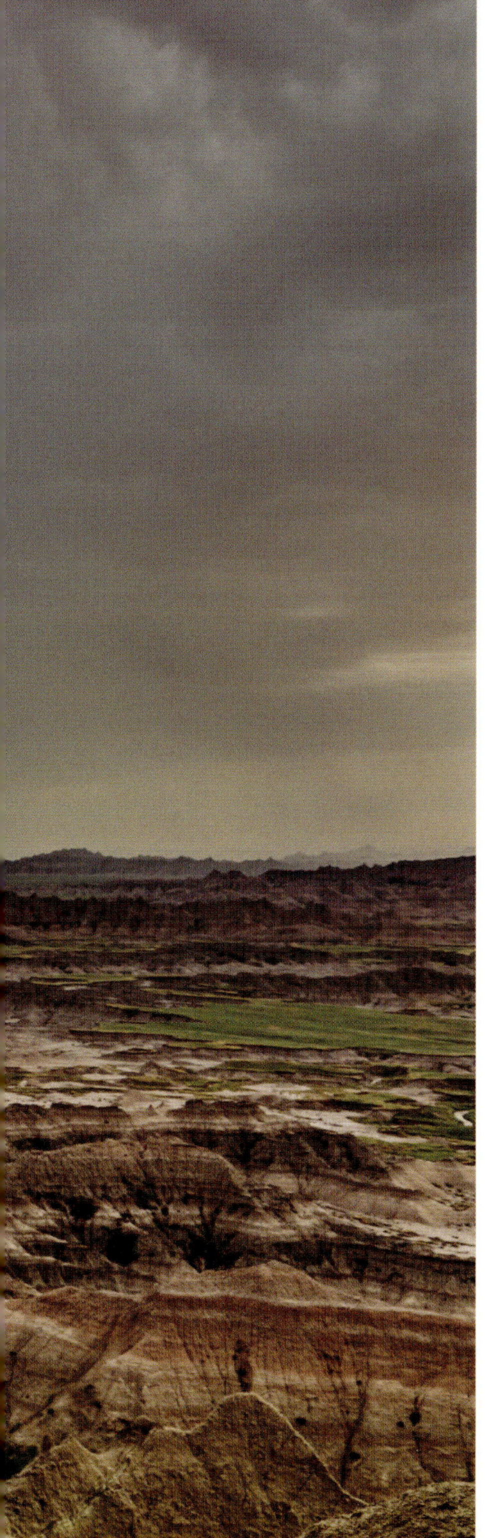

Left: A lightning bolt strikes all the way to the ground during a thunderstorm at the Pinnacles Overlook in Badlands National Park. Another feature of this park is the boardwalks that have been built in certain areas, giving access to the handicapped and wheelchair bound.

Below: Photographer Chuck Haney takes in the view from his campsite on the badlands of Upper Missouri River Breaks National Monument.

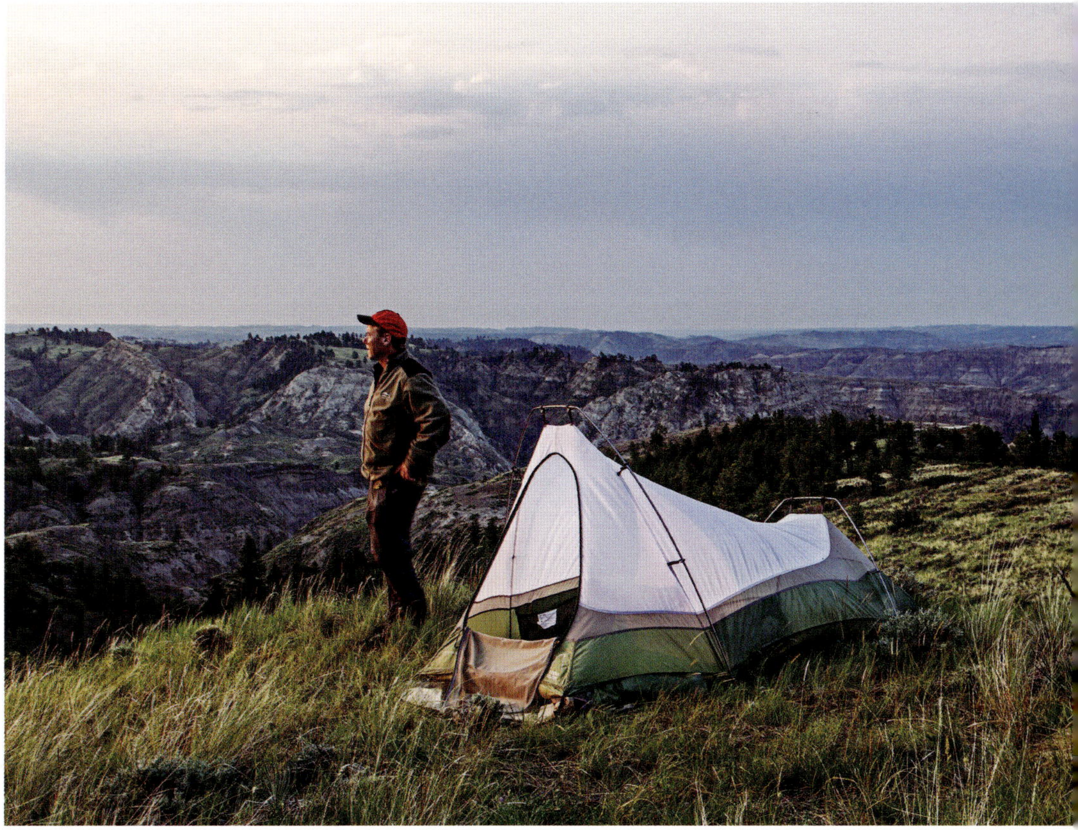

Right: Hikers explore an old homestead at Gist Bottom on Upper Missouri River Breaks National Monument. The American explorer Meriwether Lewis called this country "scenes of visionary enchantment," and the description still holds true today.

Below: A family of black-tailed prairie dogs *(Cynomys ludovicianus)* gathers around the family's hole. Common in the badlands, they live in colonies, or "towns," that usually contain thousands of individuals, generally feeding on grasses and shrubs.

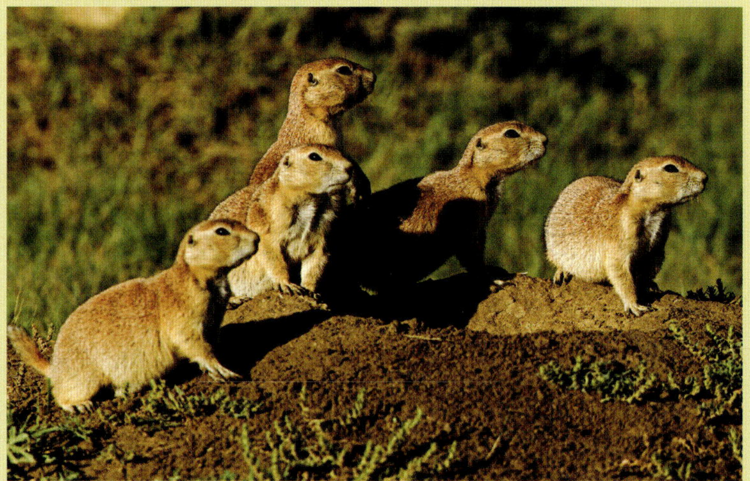

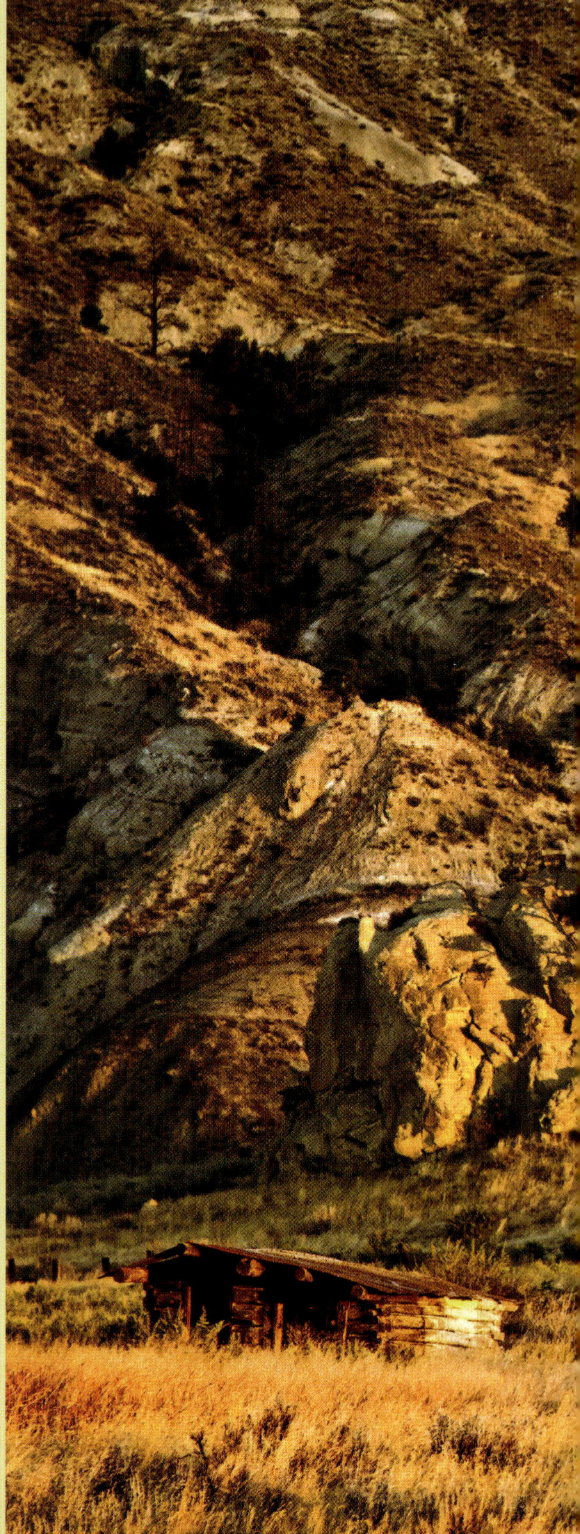

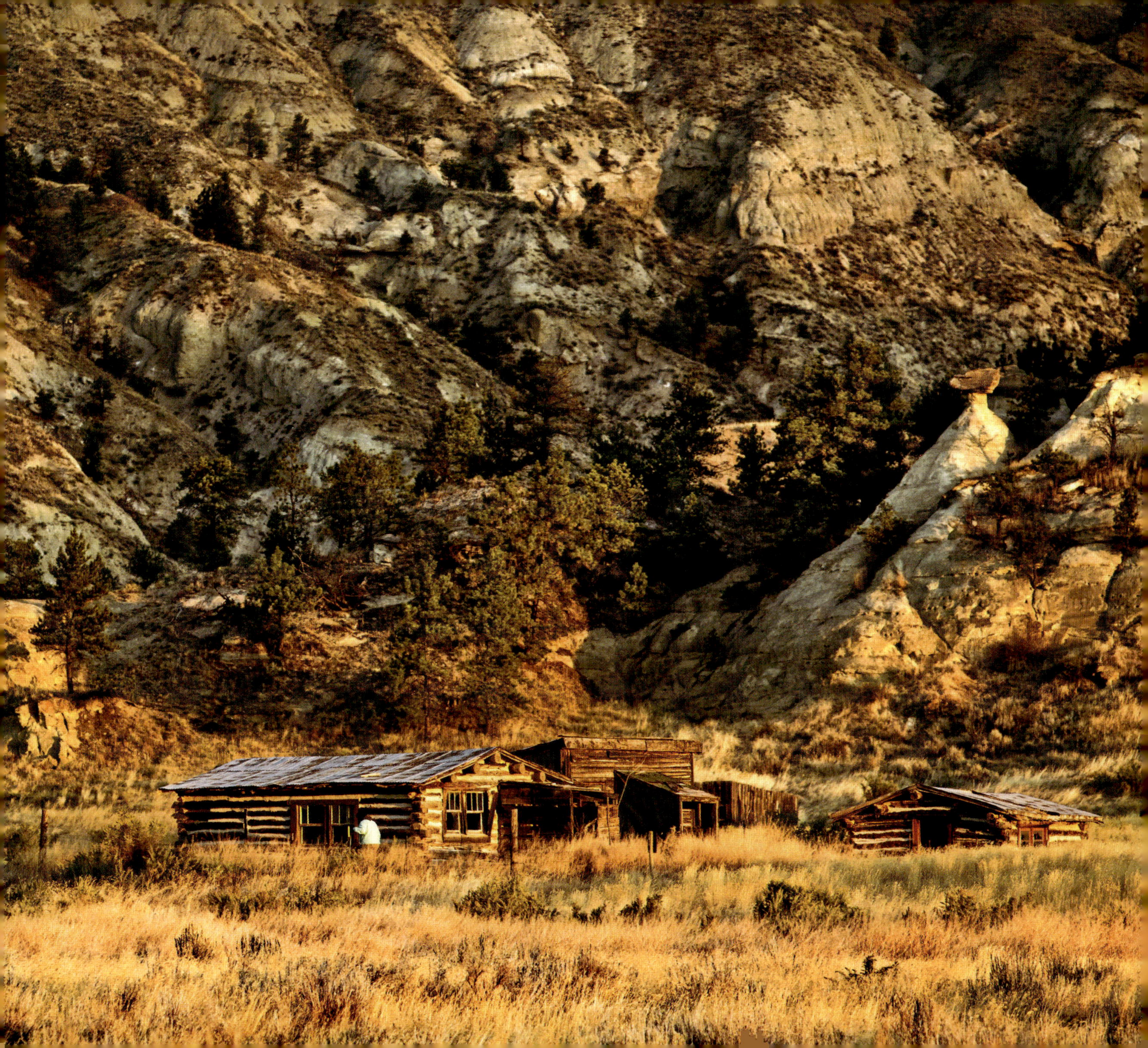

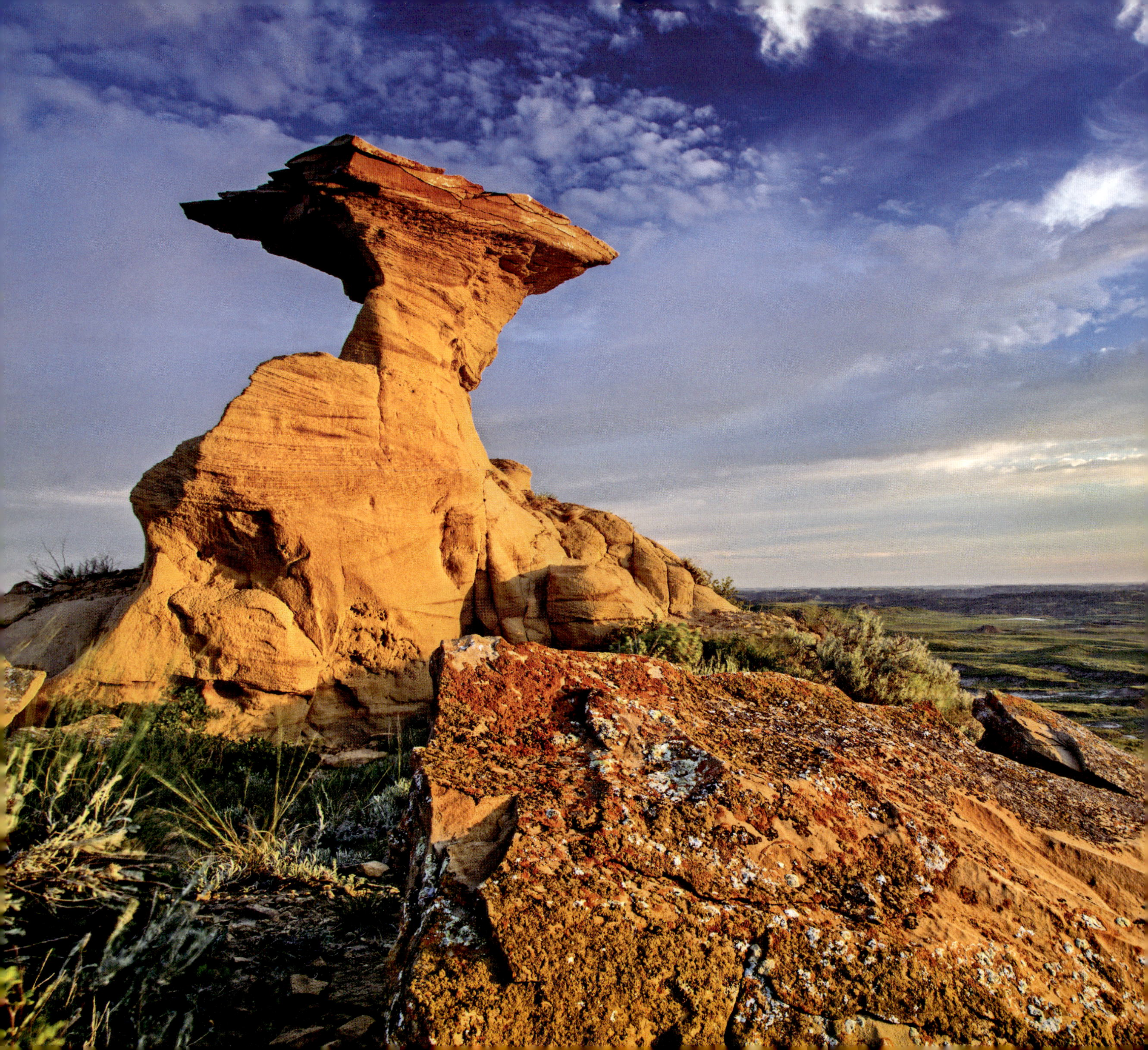

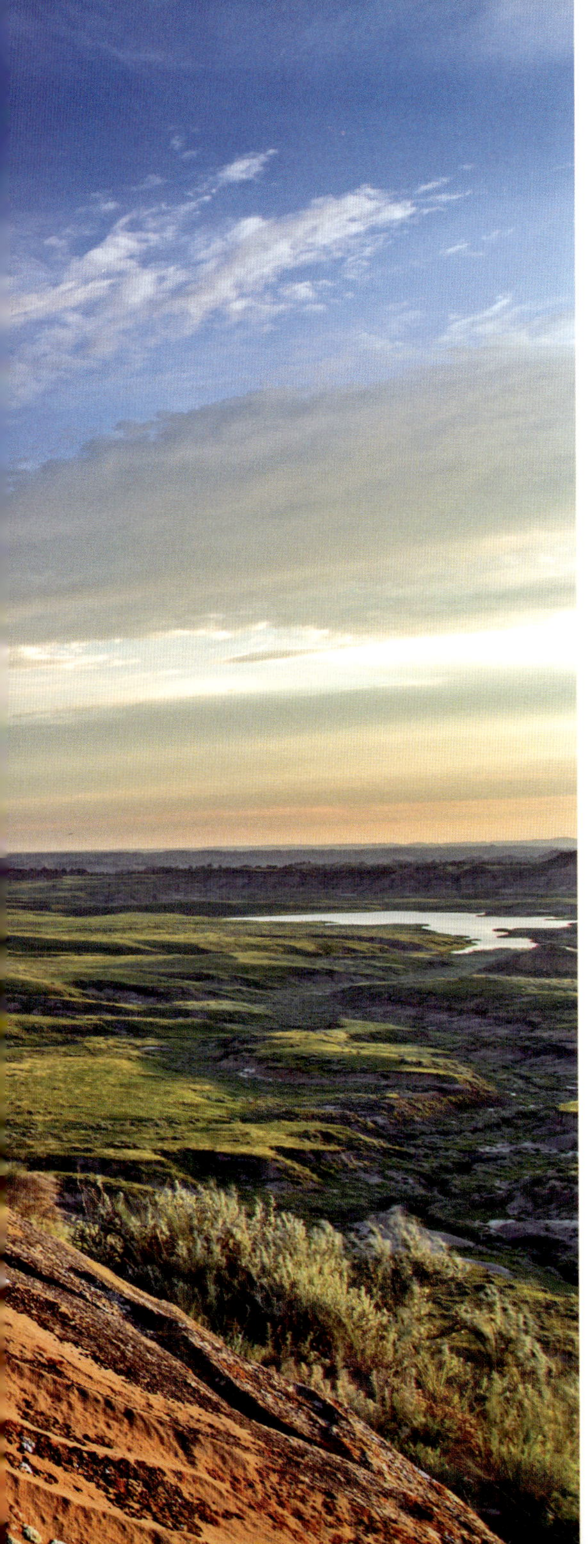

Left: A caprock sandstone formation extends skyward above a long expanse of short-grass prairie in the Hell Creek badlands of Montana's Garfield County. This region is a paleontologist's dream, featuring some of the richest fossil sites and beds in the world, which tell of the ancient tropical world that was once here.

Below: The Hudson-Meng Bison Kill site is a huge fossil bed located in the Oglala National Grassland of western Nebraska and 12 miles northwest of Crawford. Containing the 10,000-year-old remains of around 600 bison, it was a frequent hunting ground for early North American man. The site was originally excavated by Dr. Larry Agenbroad of nearby Chadron State College in the 1970s.

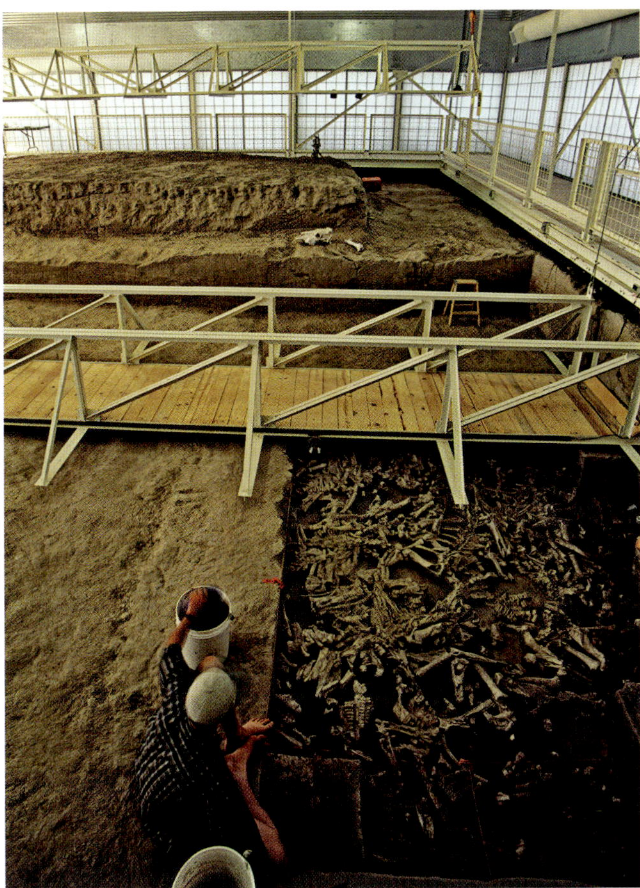

Right: The fog disappears at sunrise from the River Bend Overlook in Theodore Roosevelt National Park's North Unit. With over 100 miles of backcountry trails, this park is very popular for hiking and horseback riding. The night skies provide excellent stargazing opportunities along with occasional northern lights.

Below: Flowering yucca plants *(Yucca glauca)* adorn this ridge overlooking the Fort Peck Reservoir in the Charles M. Russell National Wildlife Refuge in Montana. Fort Peck Lake is the fifth-largest artificial lake in the United States and extends 134 miles through central Montana.

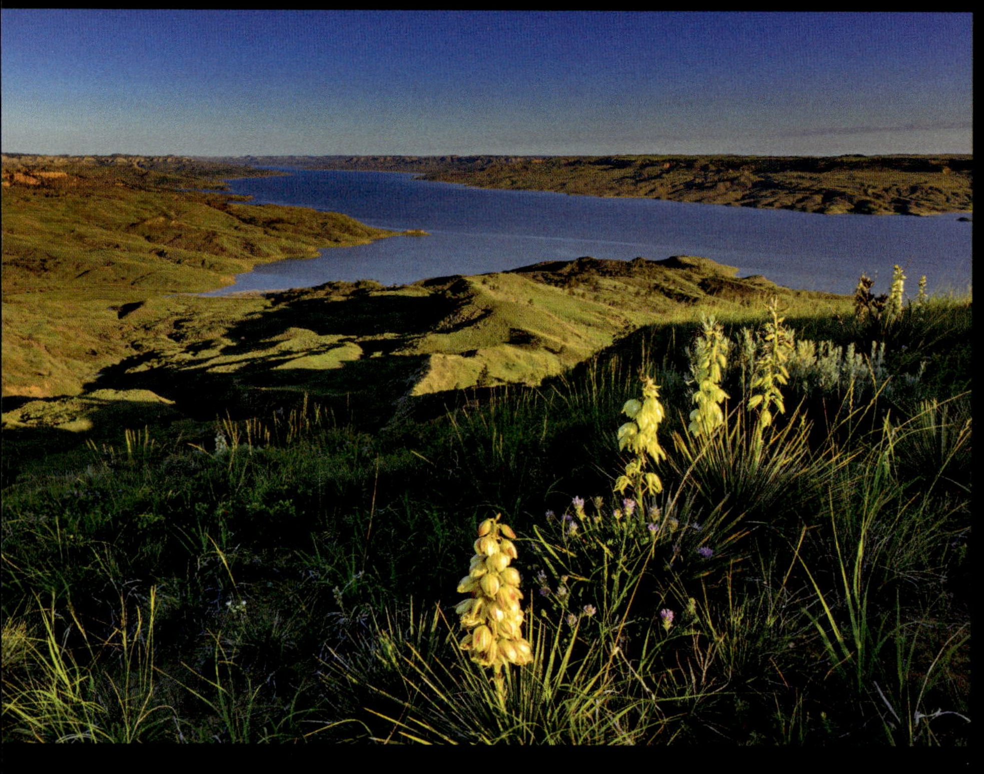

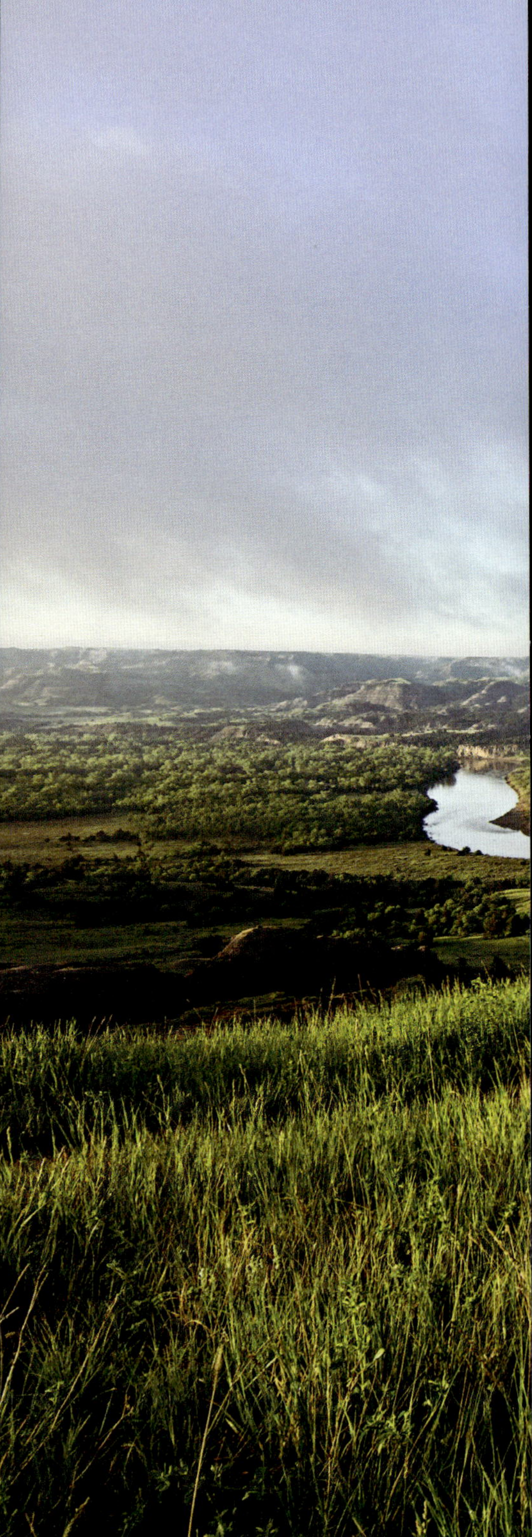

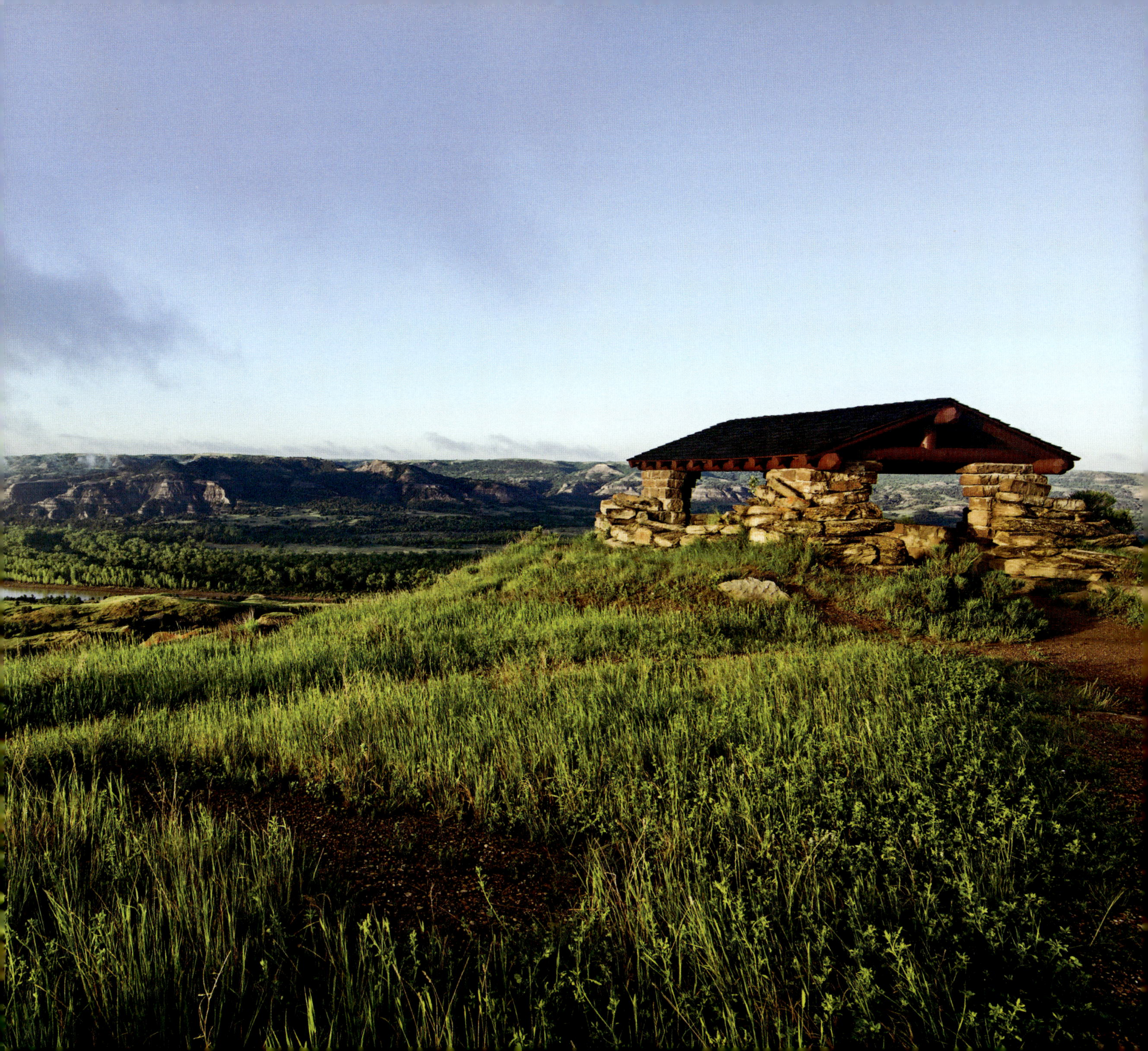

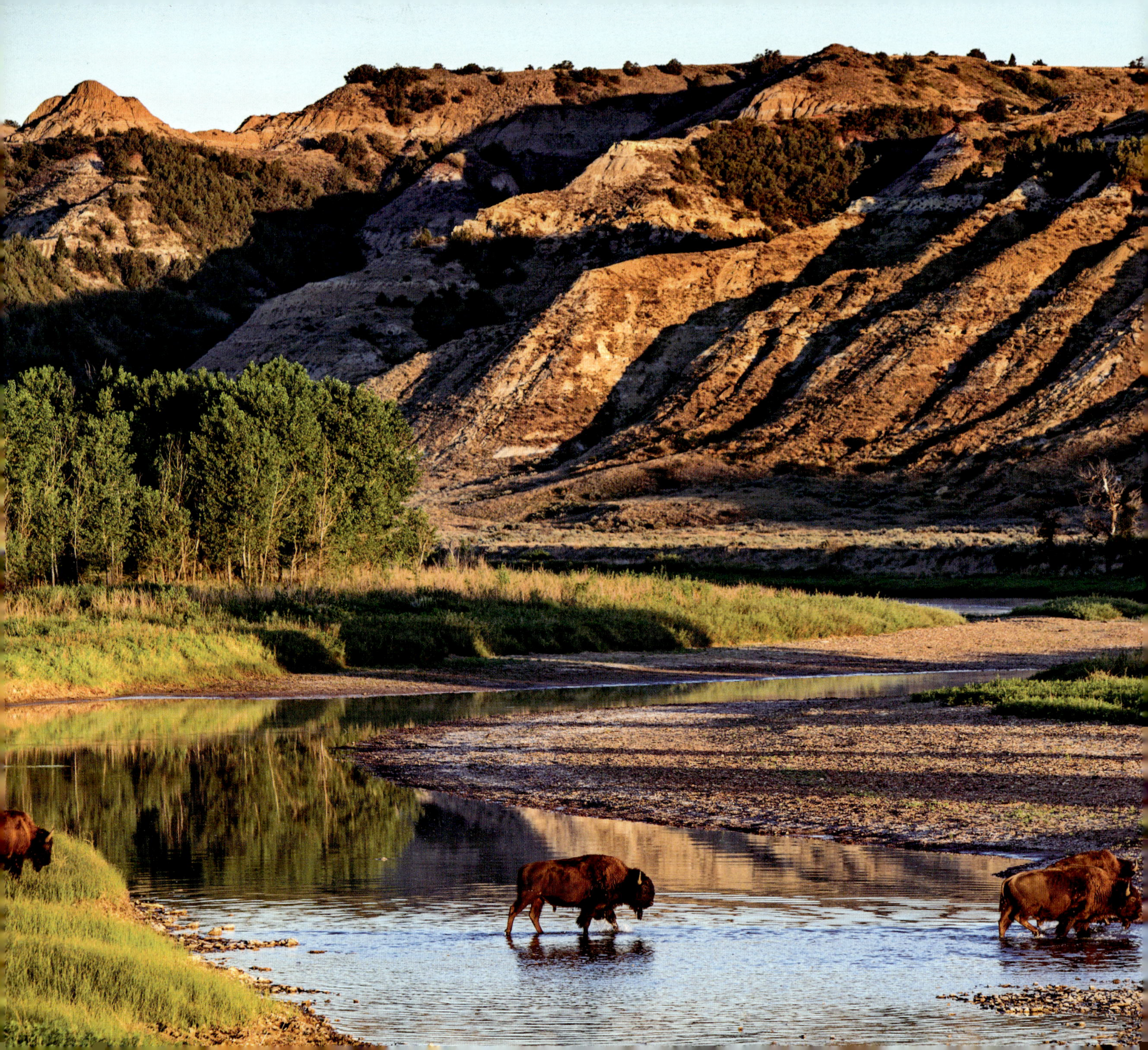

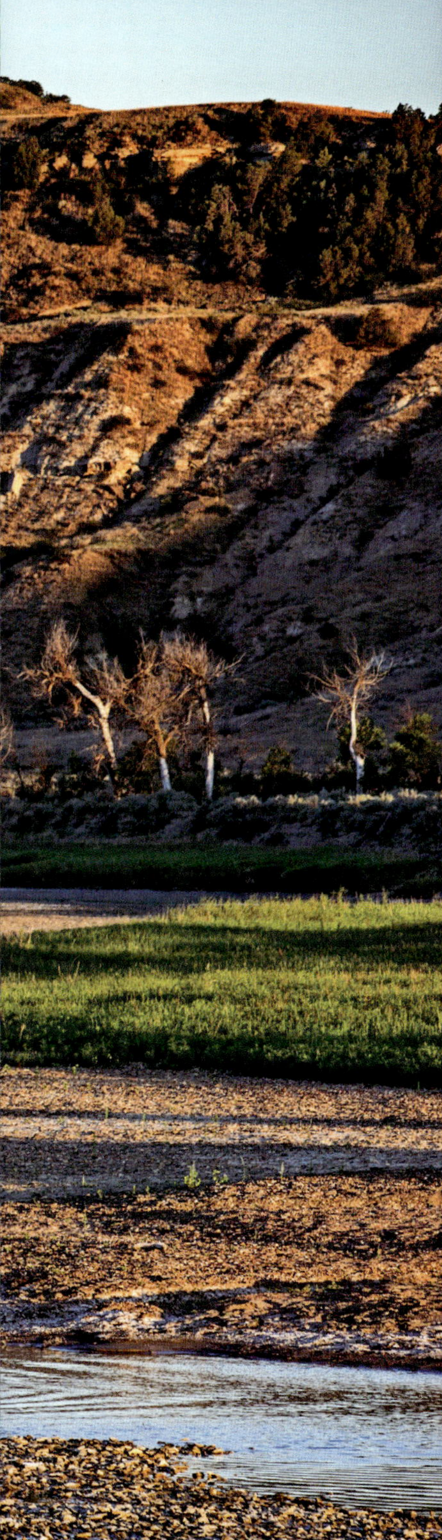

Left: Bison *(Bison bison)* cross the Little Missouri River in Theodore Roosevelt National Park. First reintroduced to the park in 1956, the population of these "lordly" animals, as Teddy Roosevelt described them, has grown to several hundred as they have strongly reestablished themselves in this rugged landscape.

Below: Morning light illuminates Chimney Rock, a prominent geological rock formation in Morrill County of western Nebraska, or the Nebraska Panhandle, as locals know it. During the mid-19th century the Rock served as a landmark for westward bound settlers along the Oregon Trail, the California Trail, and the Mormon Trail.

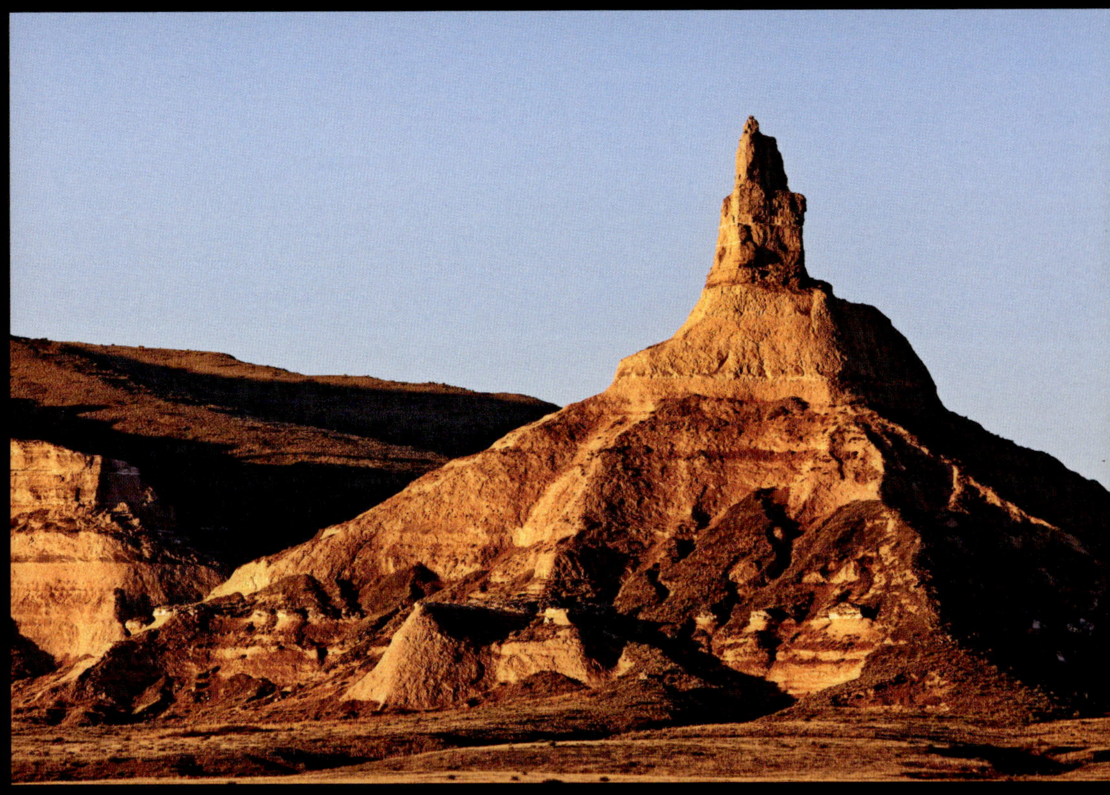

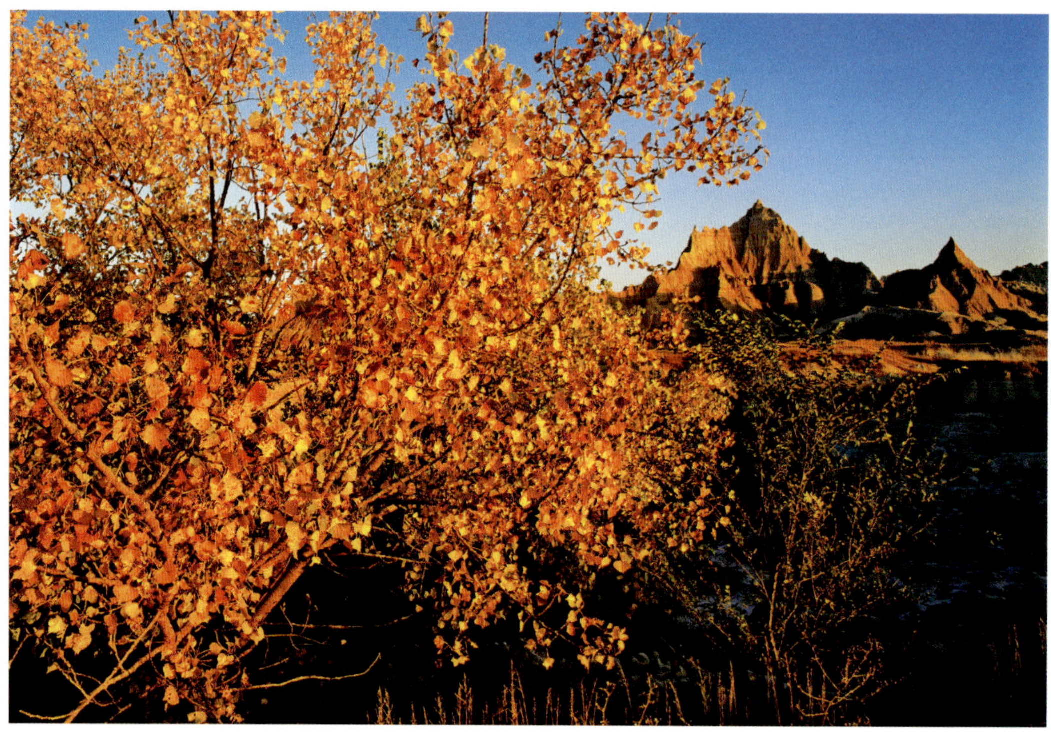

Above: Autumn color begins to decorate the landscape across the western prairies of Badlands National Park. Wet years can bring a bonanza of rich color to the flora of this otherwise semi-arid region.

Right: Fossilized tree stumps like this one are some of the many sights to experience on a trek into Theodore Roosevelt National Park's Petrified Forest Wilderness and its geological past. This site is located in the remote northwest corner of the South Unit and is accessible by two different trails.

Far right: A mushroom rock formation rises before a meandering Missouri River in its Wild and Scenic section in central Montana. For over 12,000 years, people have depended on this fabled waterway as a source for sustenance and transportation.

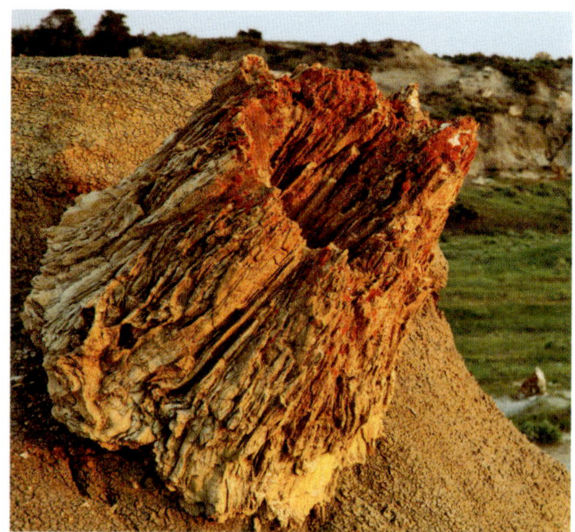

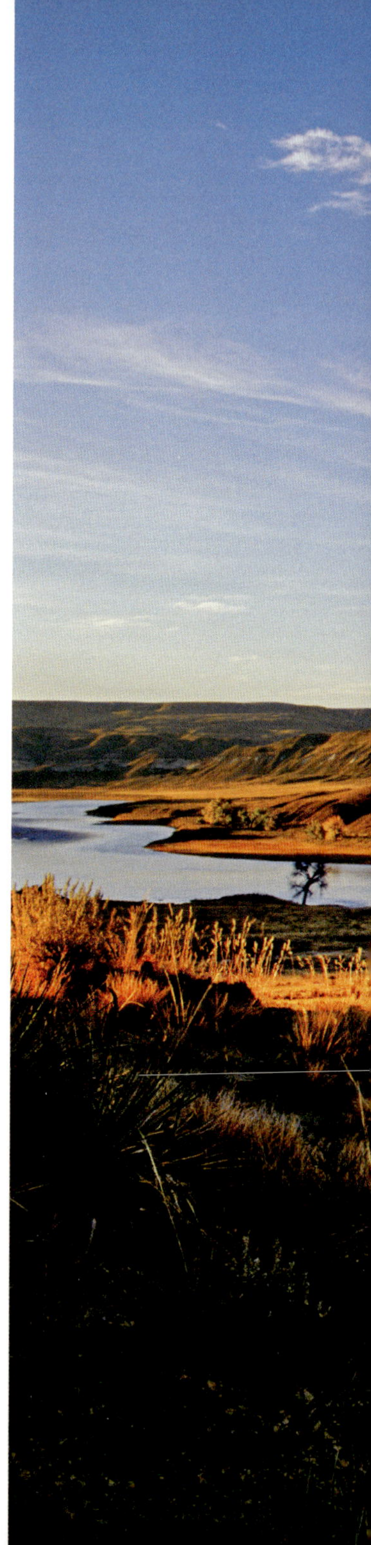

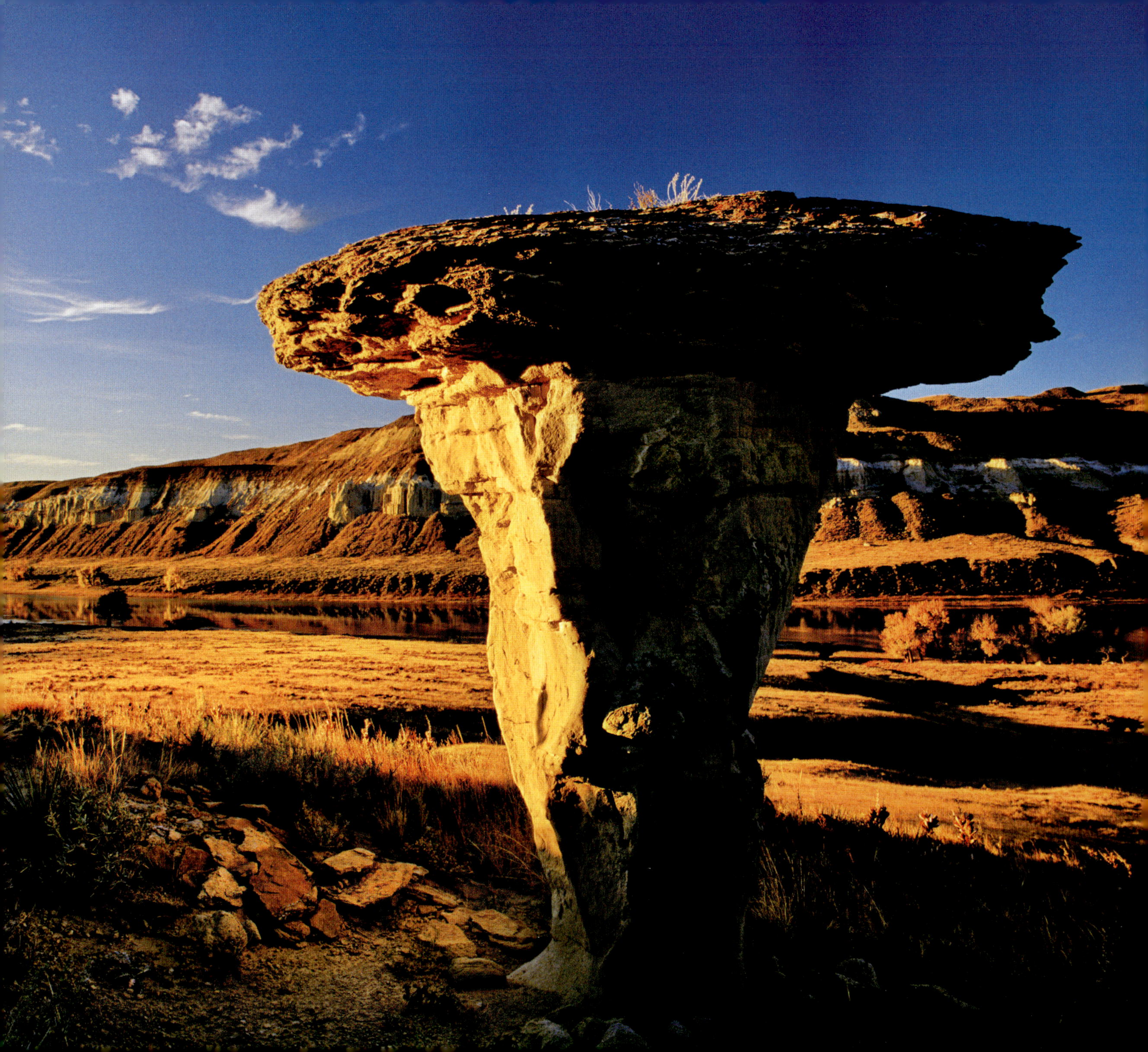

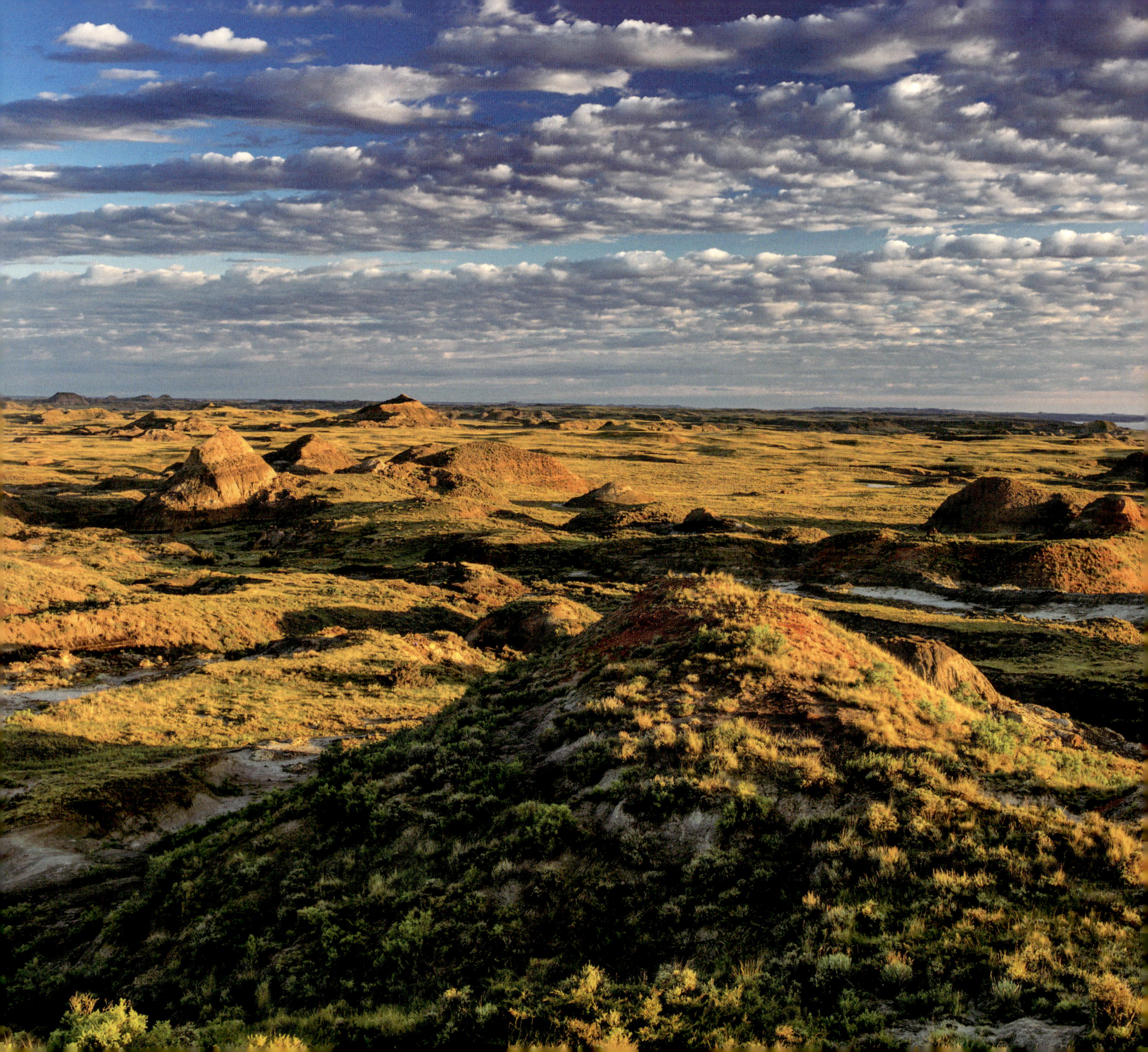

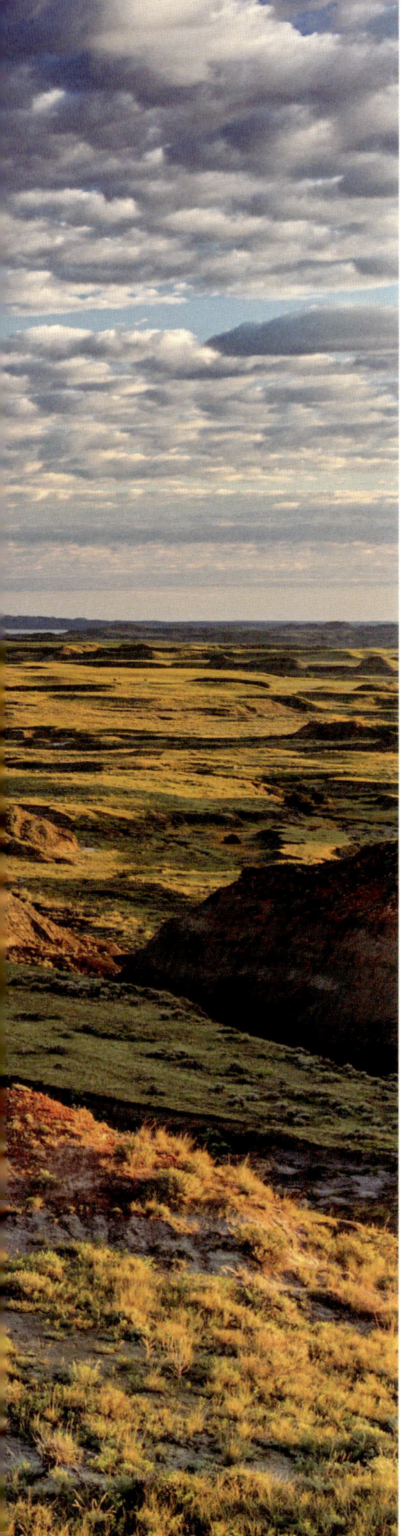

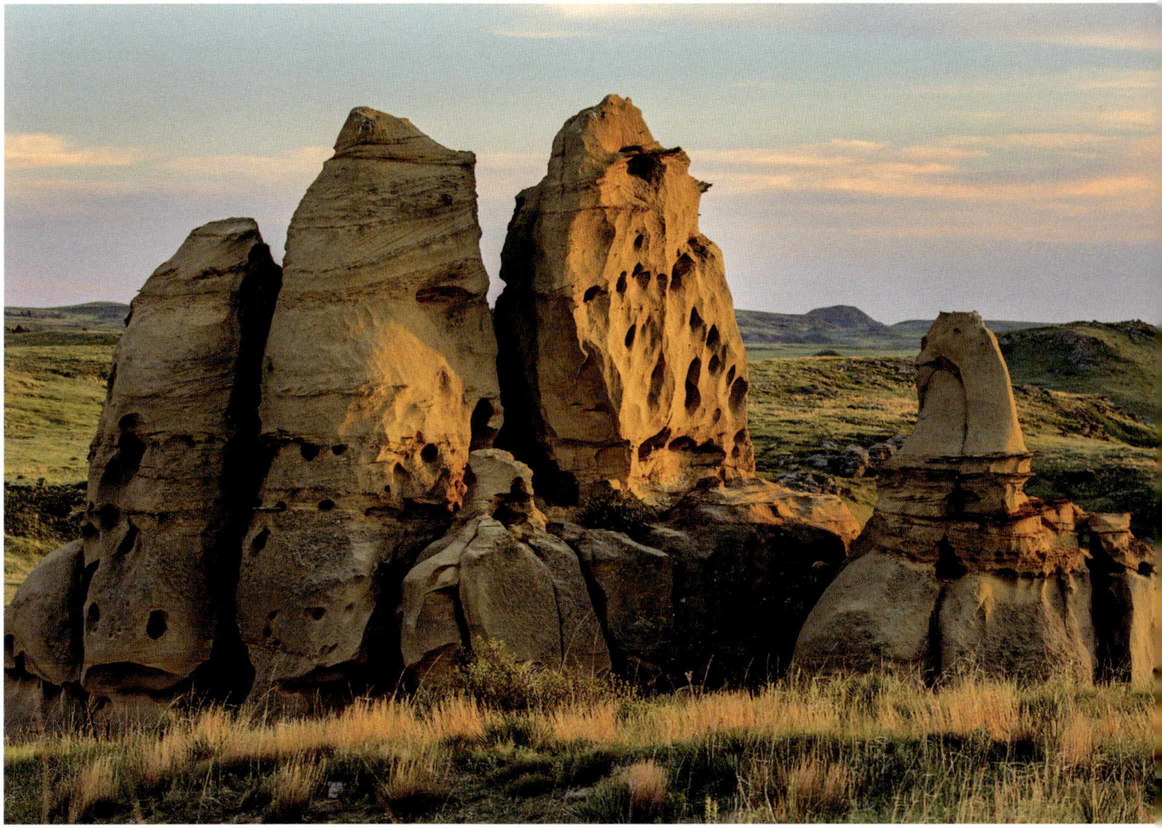

Above: A morning sun near Ekalaka, Montana, lights some of the fascinating sandstone pillars of Medicine Rocks State Park. Considered a sacred place by Native Americans, this park is about 330 acres in size and is named for its eerie rock formations with holes and tunnels through them. Theodore Roosevelt described Medicine Rocks "as fantastically beautiful a place as I have ever seen."

Left: Daybreak light stretches across the colorful badlands adjacent to the Fort Peck Reservoir. The reservoir is Montana's largest body of water and is surrounded by the one million-acre Charles M. Russell National Wildlife Refuge.

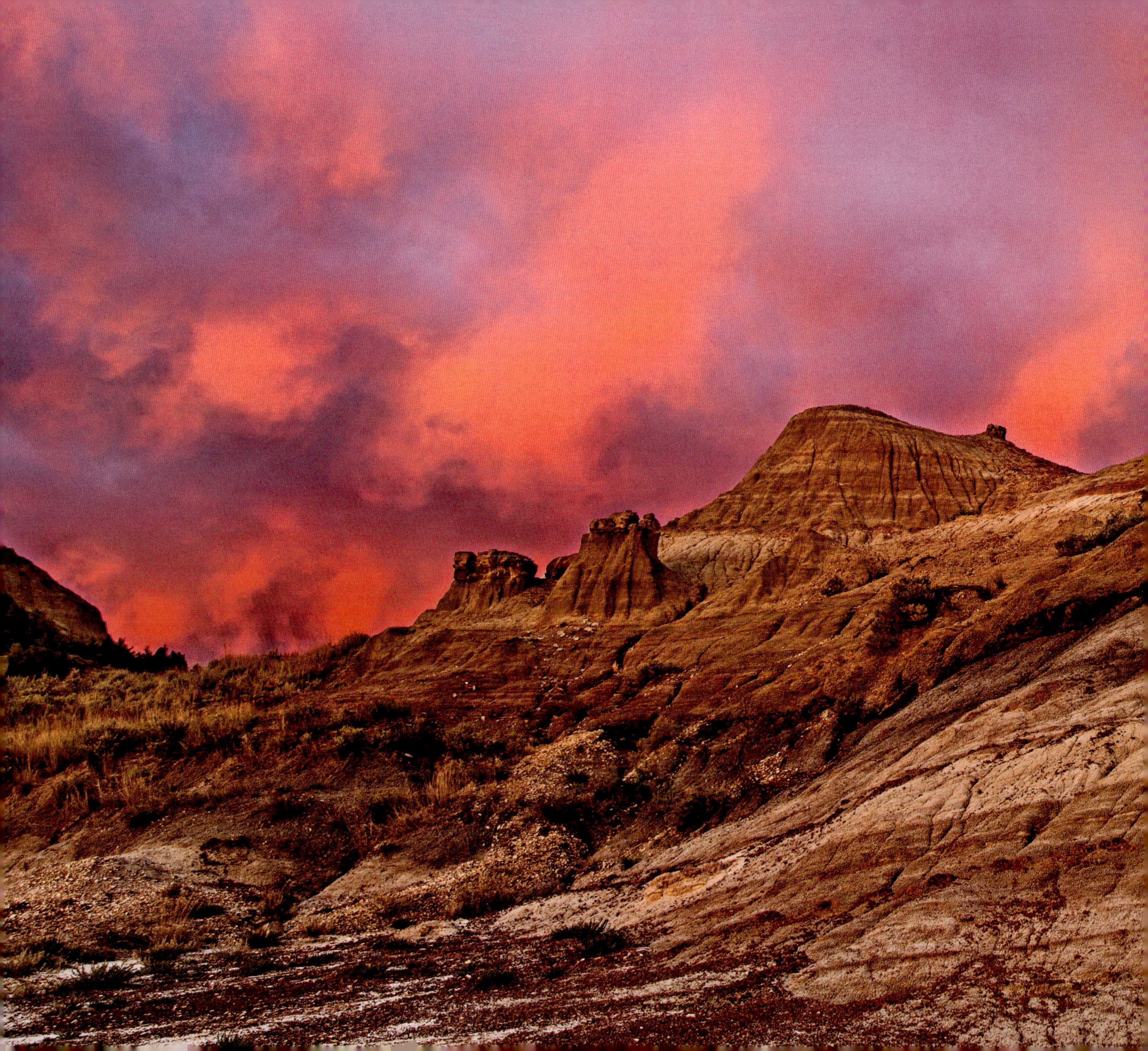

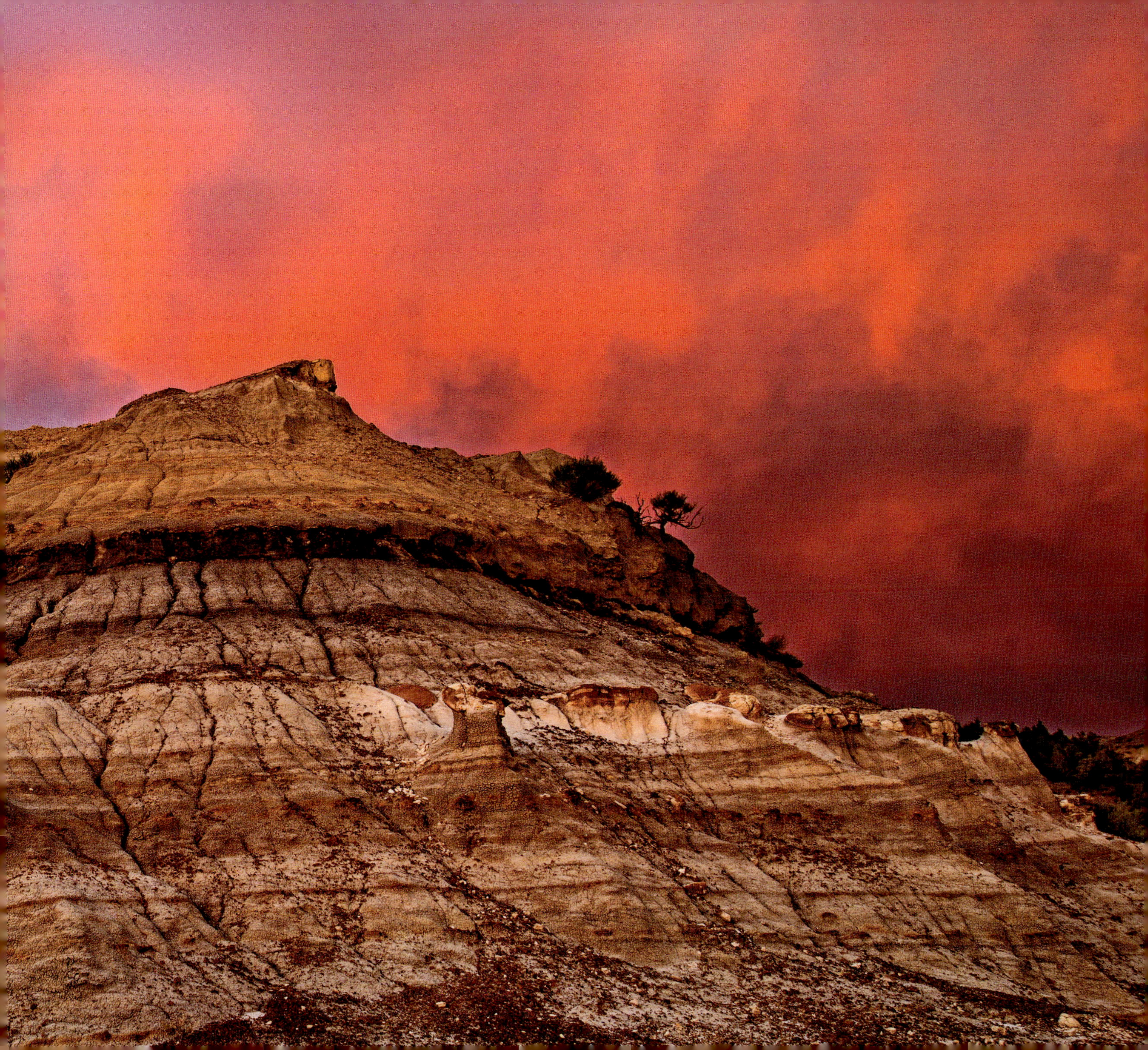

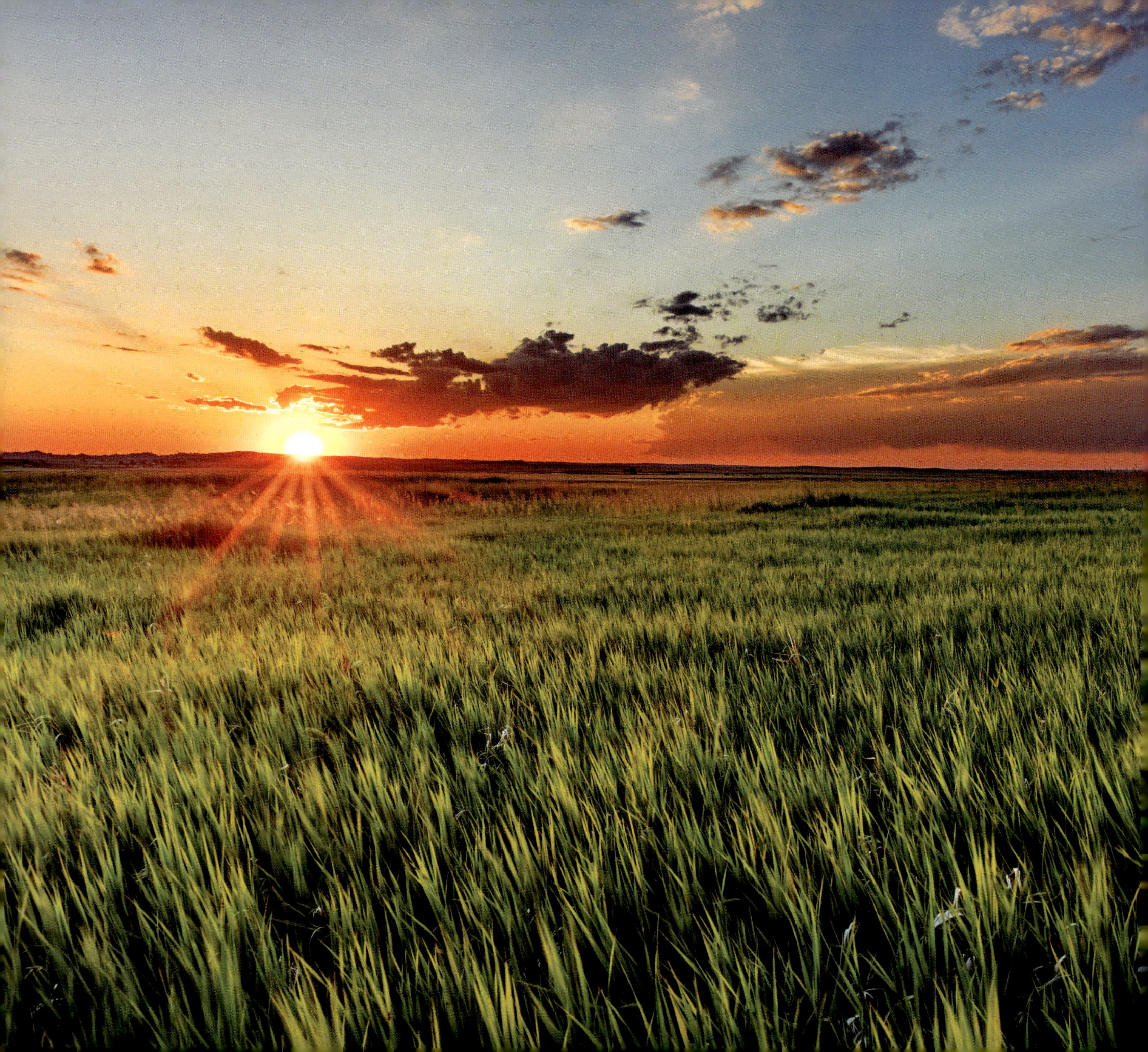

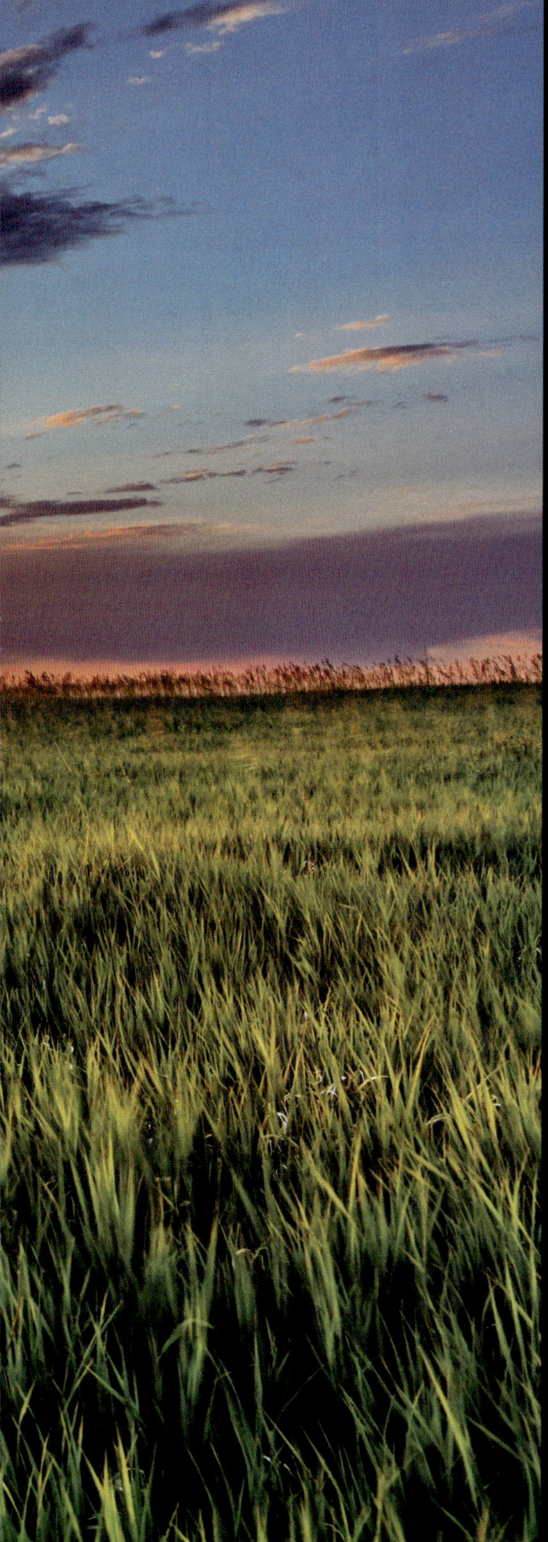

Previous pages: Fiery clouds and color embellish this dawn sky over the bluffs and badlands of Theodore Roosevelt National Park. Dramatic landscapes like this one, plus a rugged and strenuous ranch life, would inspire a young Teddy Roosevelt to later shape a conservation policy from which we still benefit even today.

Left: A setting sun takes a last look over the grasslands of Badlands National Park near Wall. This park includes one of the largest expanses of mixed-grass prairie left in the United States. Containing both ankle-high and waist-high grasses, these prairies represent a transitional zone from the humid, tall grass prairies of southern Minnesota and Iowa to the more arid short-grass prairies that lie west of here.

Below: A sharp-tailed grouse hen *(Tympanuchus phasianellus)* pokes through the grass at the American Prairie Reserve near Malta, Montana. One of the most striking of the prairie birds, the grouse still exists in high numbers across much of the Great Plains. Each spring these birds gather on leks, or booming grounds, for a fascinating courtship display.

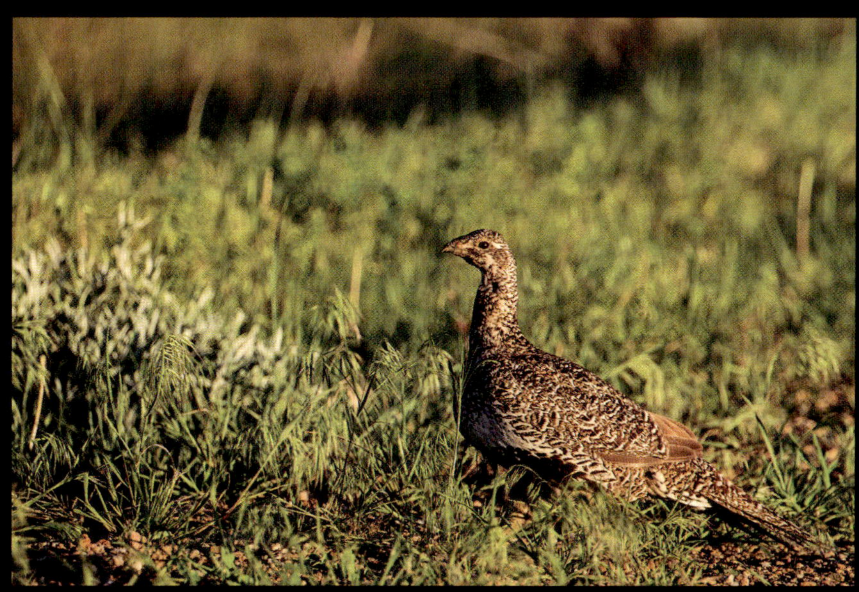

Right: A balanced rock stands atop a bluff on the Yellowstone River Breaks that overlook the river near Sidney, Montana. The Yellowstone River is another major tributary of the Missouri River, running 692 miles. It flows through the Yellowstone River watershed, a river basin containing a system of rivers that form tributaries to the Missouri in North Dakota.

Below: These layers of sandstone in Theodore Roosevelt National Park tell the story of the region's geological past.

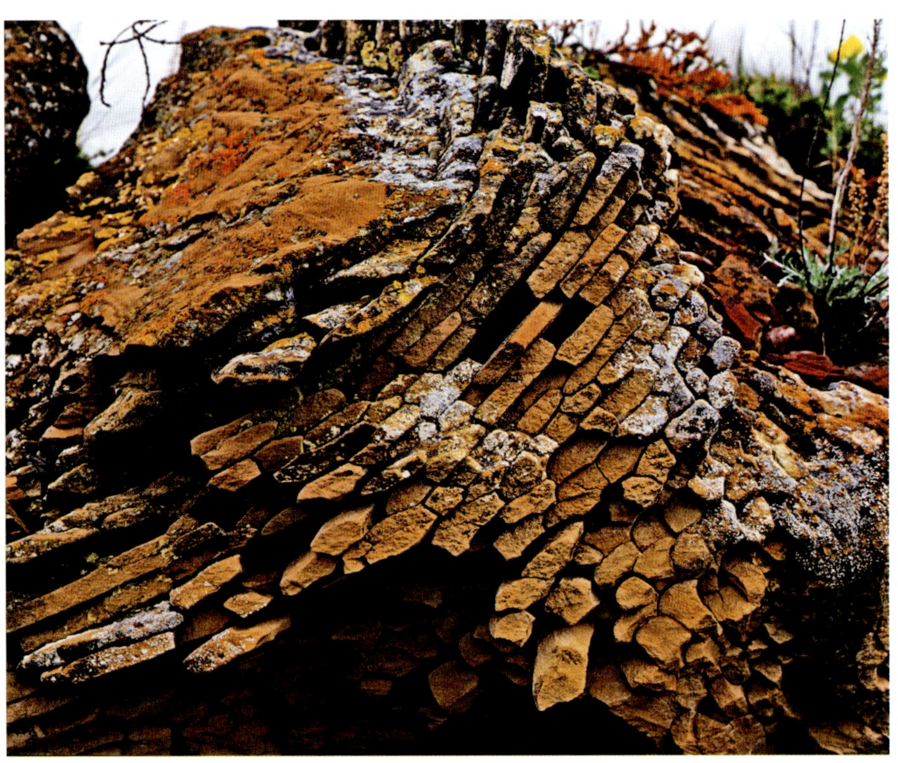

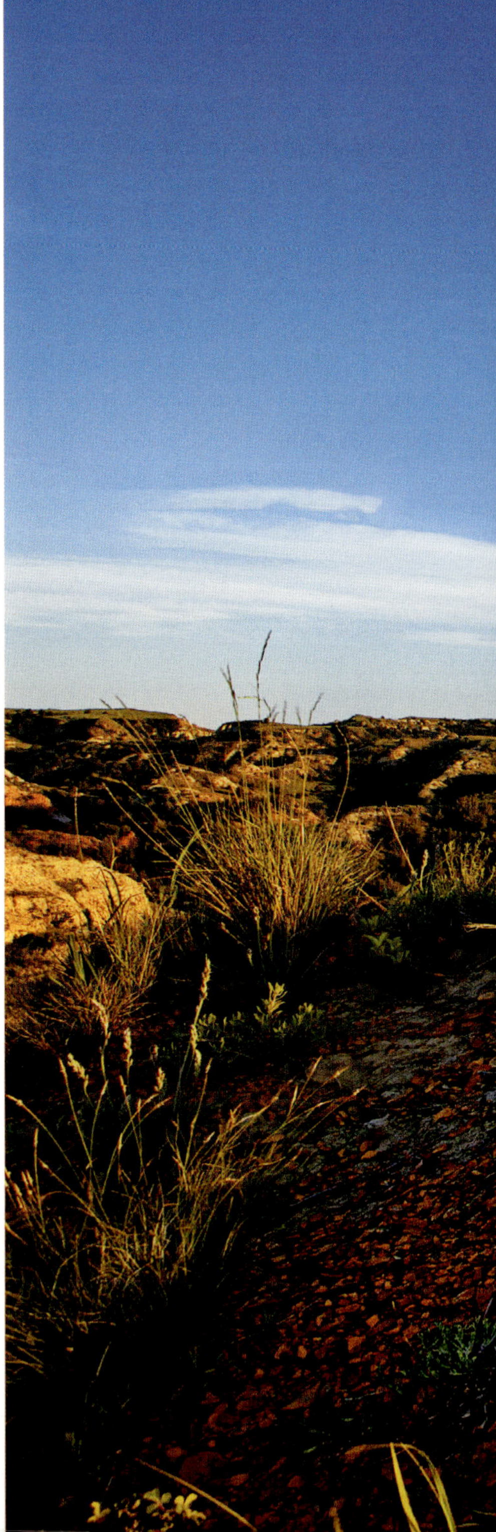

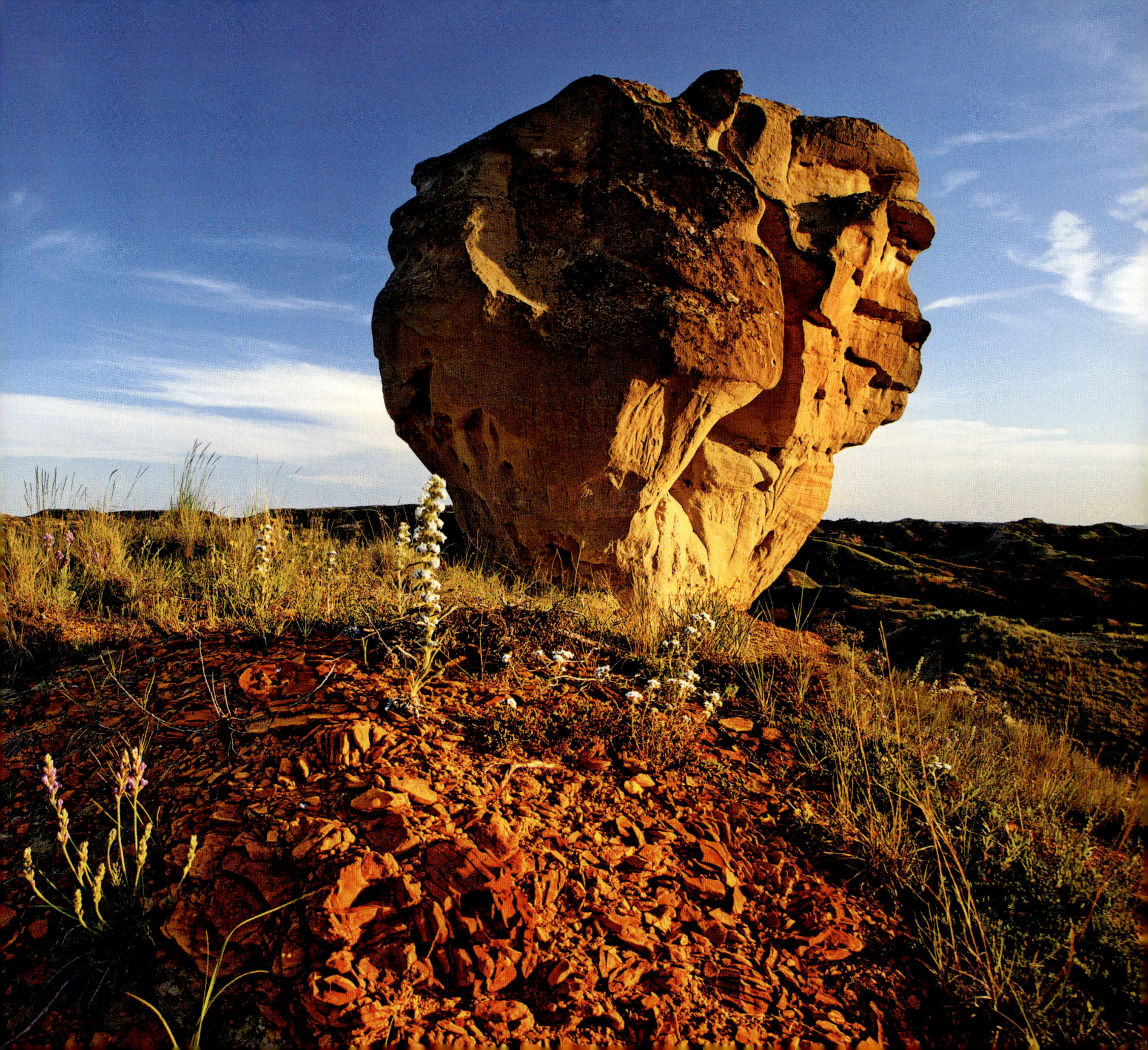

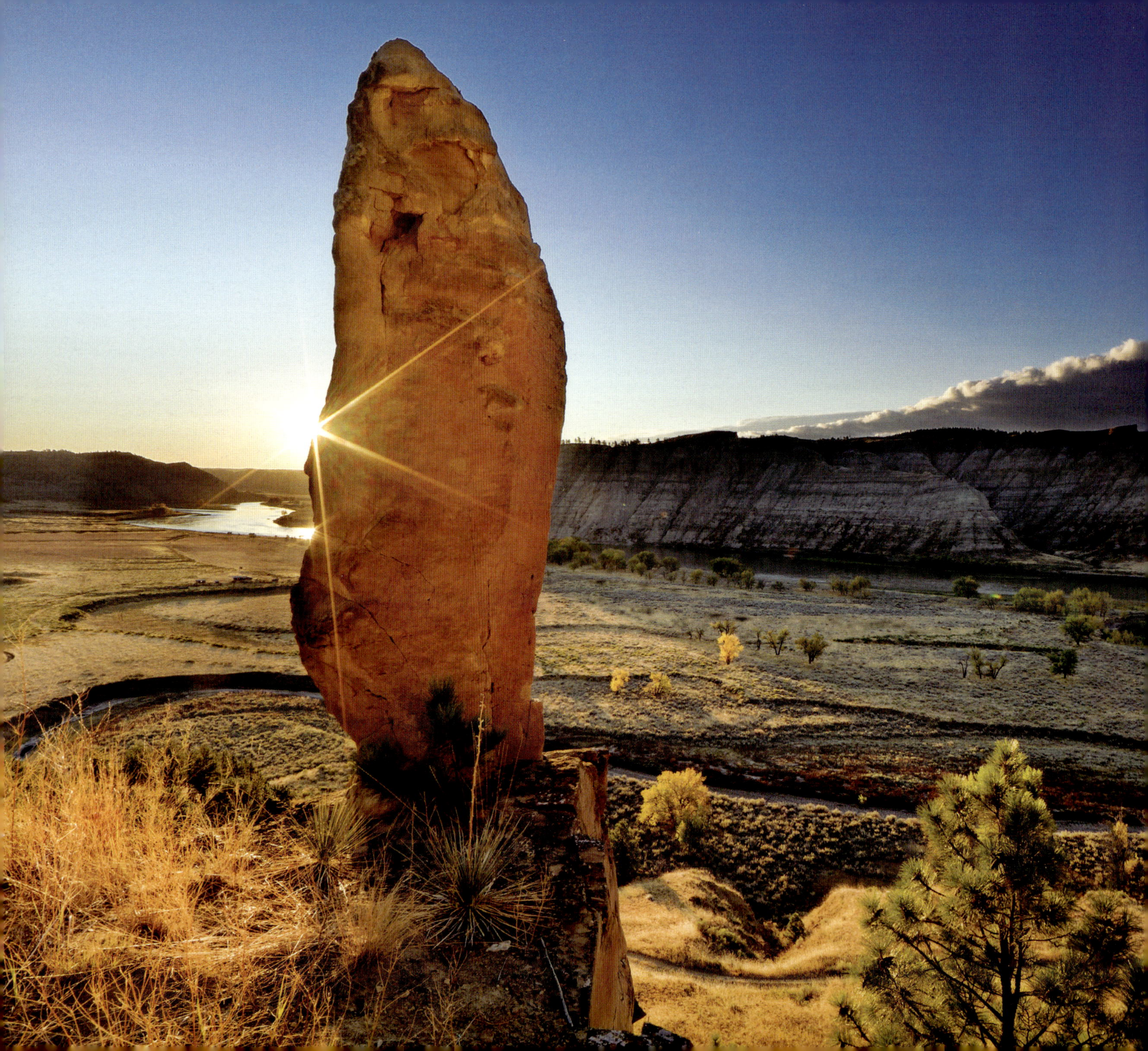

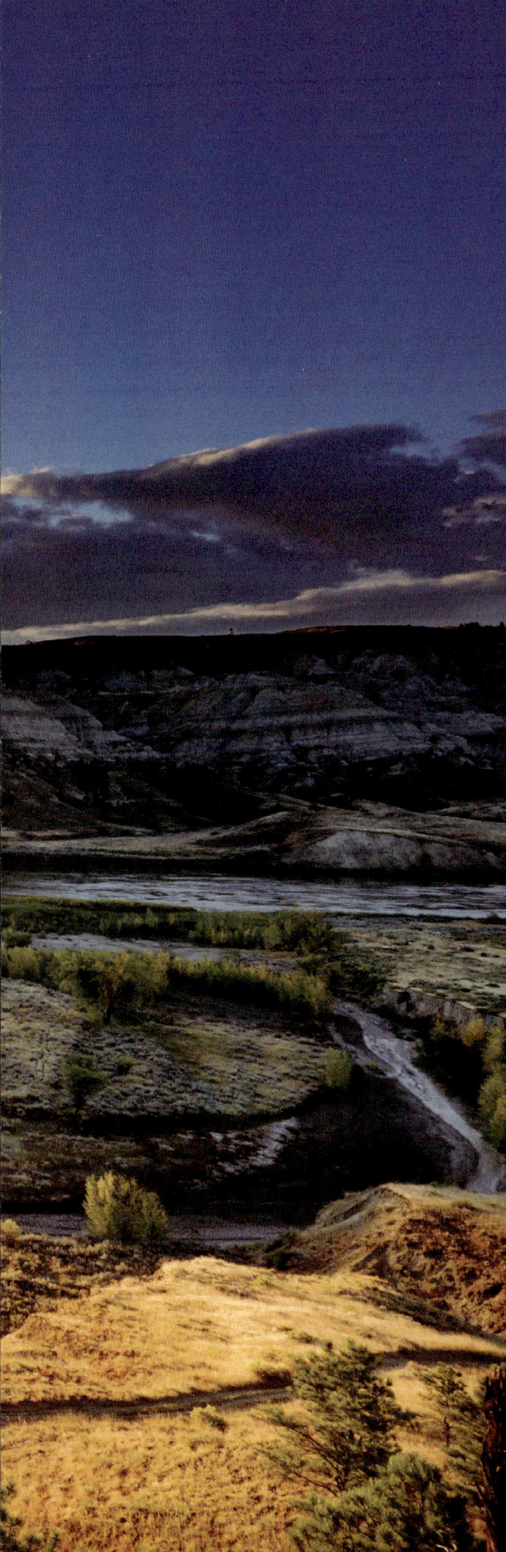

Left: A rising sun peeks from behind Pinnacle Rock in this river ravine where Bullwhacker Creek joins the Missouri River at the Upper Missouri River Breaks National Monument. "The Breaks" are a series of badland areas defined by rocky outcroppings, steep bluffs, and grassy plains. This section of the Missouri has also been designated a Wild and Scenic River.

Below: Another of Theodore Roosevelt National Park's more unusual sights is the Cannonball Concretions of the North Unit. A concretion is a hard, compact mass of matter that is formed by the precipitation of mineral cement within the spaces between particles. Concretions are often ovoid or spherical in shape, taking on the look of a cannonball or bowling ball.

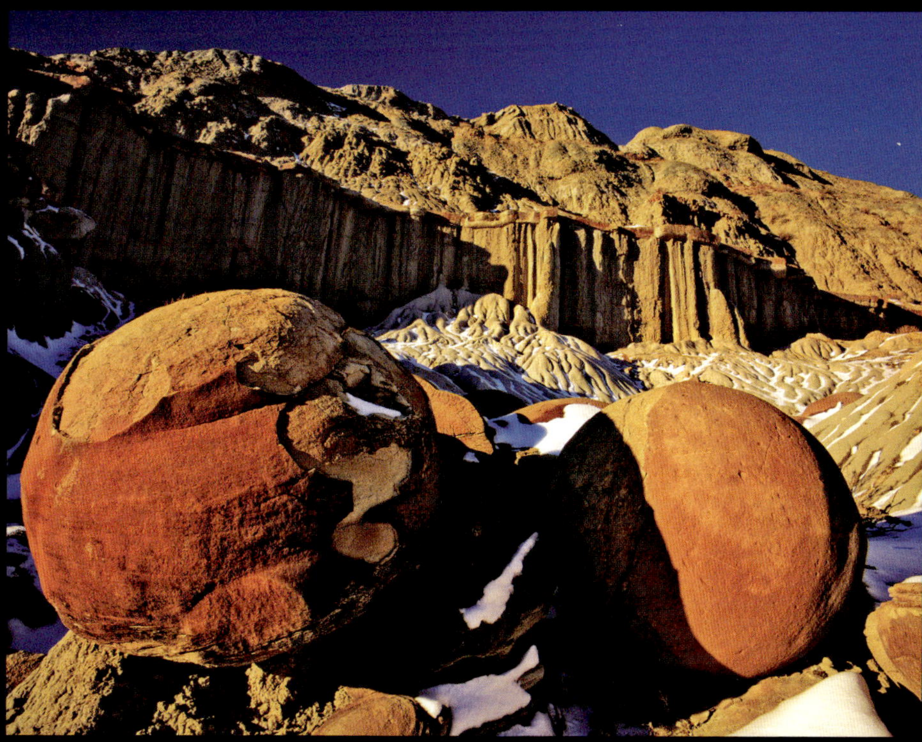

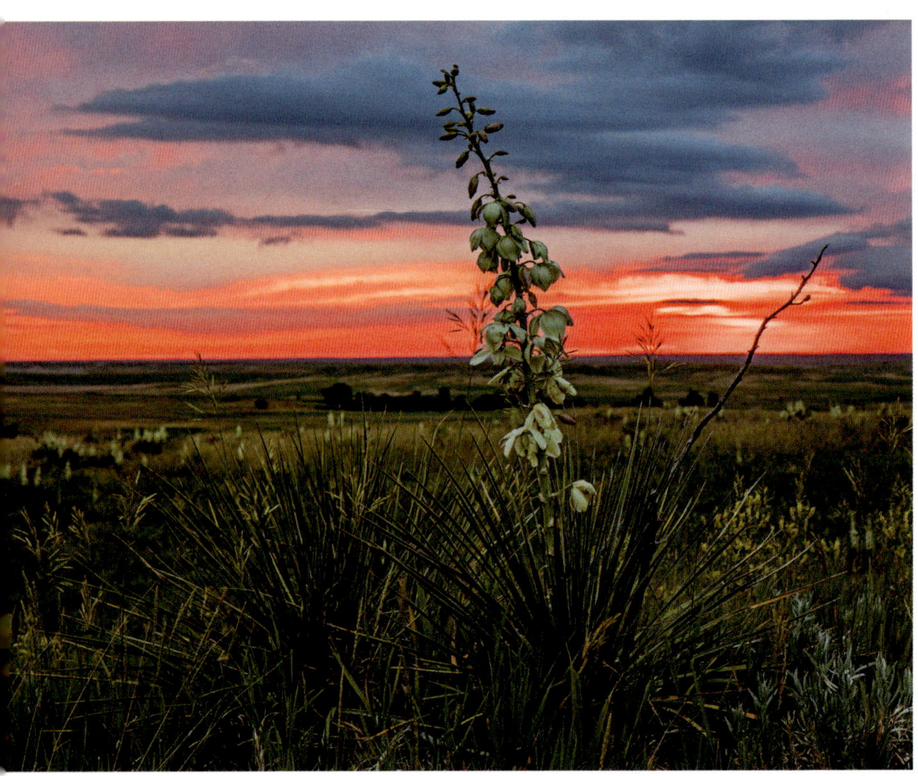

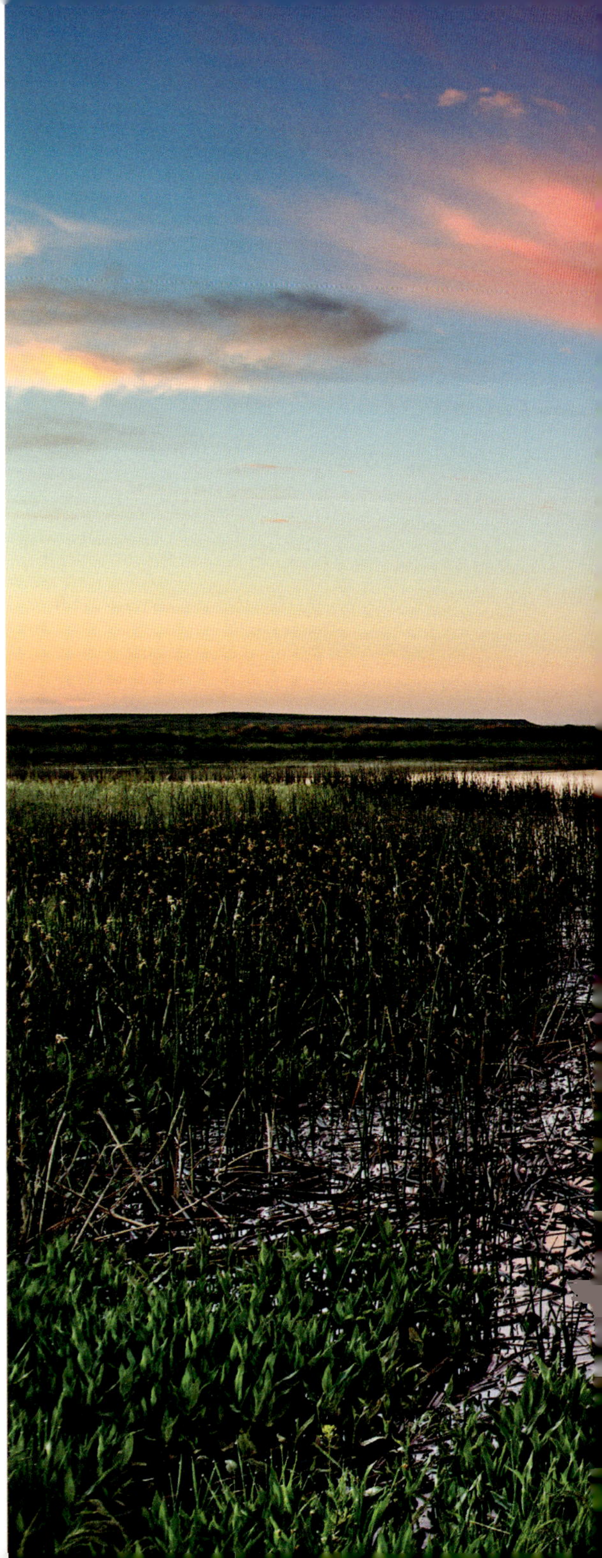

Above: A yucca plant *(Yucca glauca)* lends its beauty to a stunning sunrise in Badlands National Park. Blooming across much of the high plains during June, this plant was used extensively by Native Americans, who made sandals from the leaf fibers, food from the white flower petals, and soaps and medications from the roots.

Right: Dawn light brings out the colors of a beautiful big sky as they are reflected in this prairie pond on Hell Creek badlands. Nearby fossil beds yielded the most complete Hadrosaurid (duck-billed) dinosaur yet to be found.

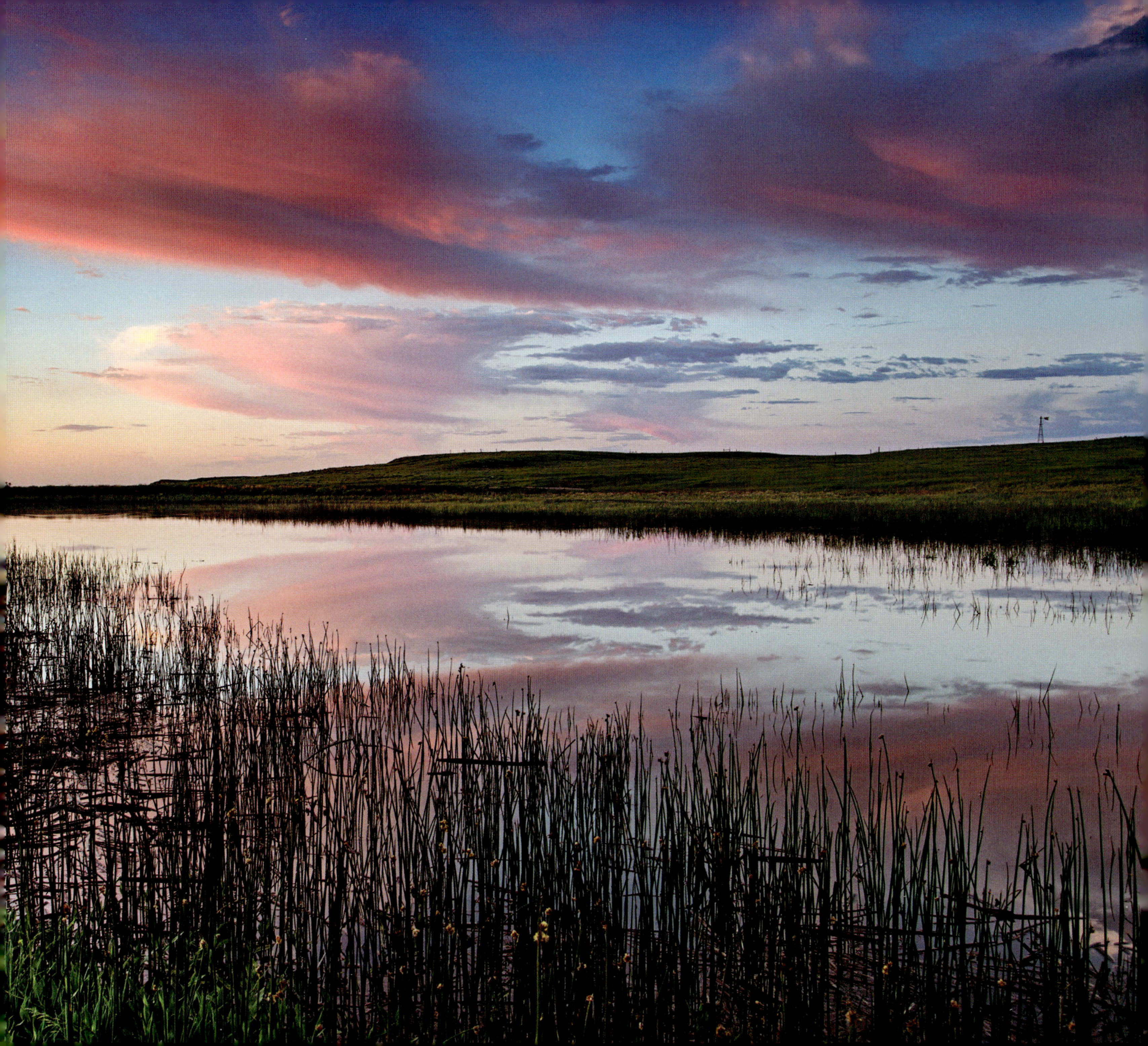

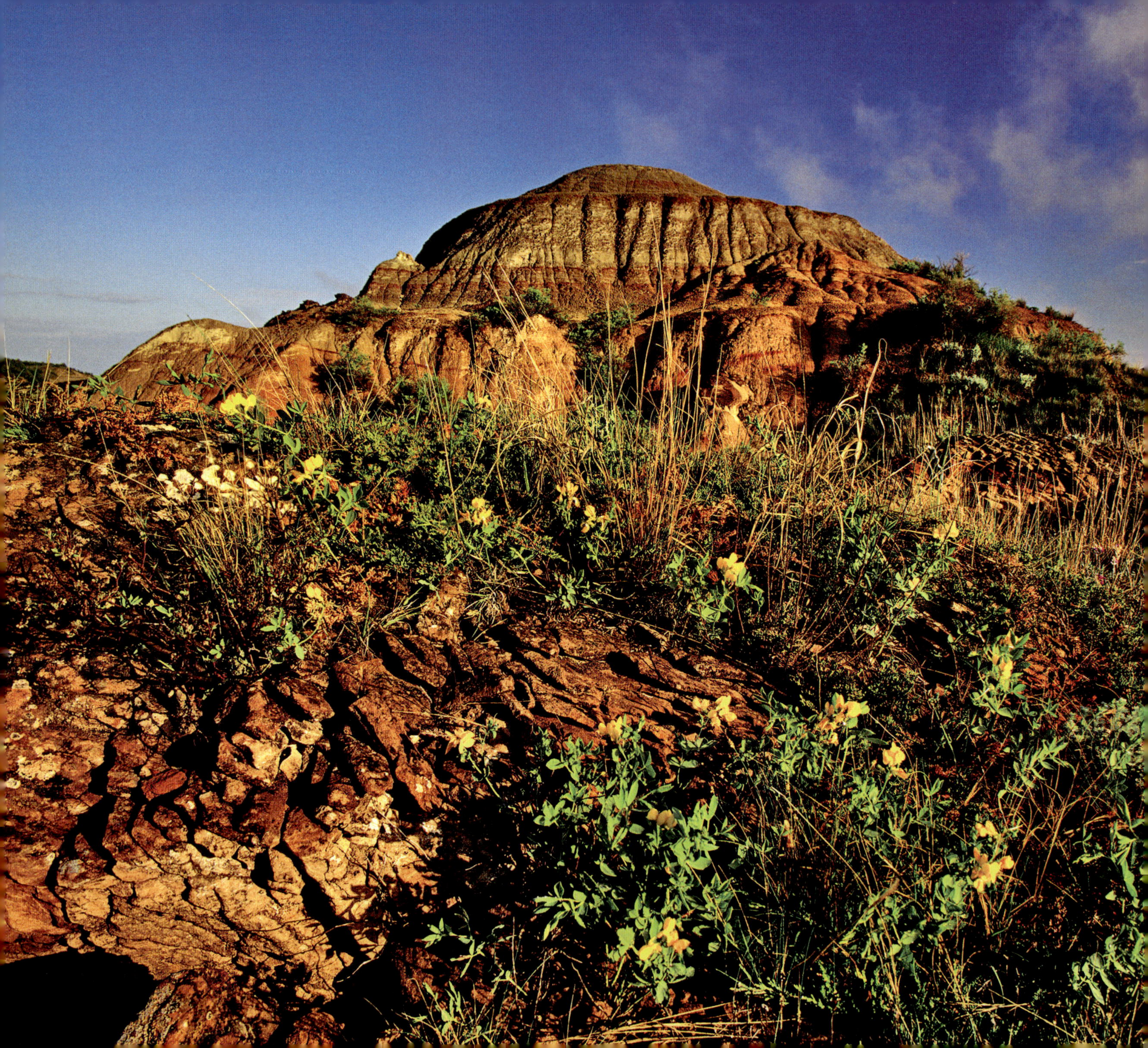

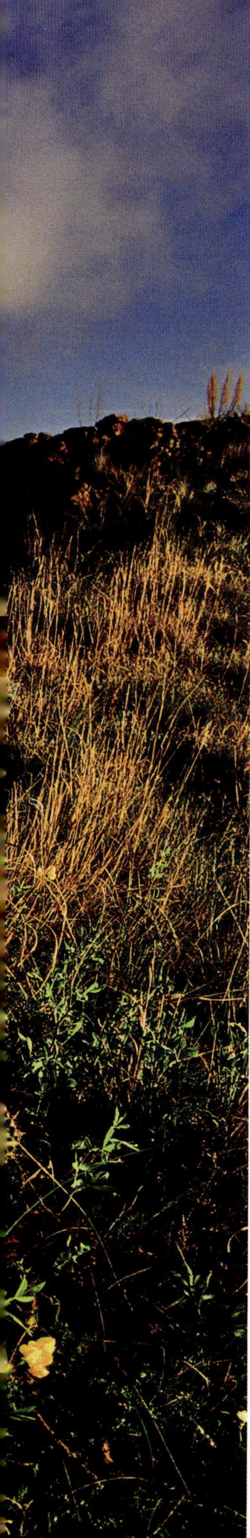

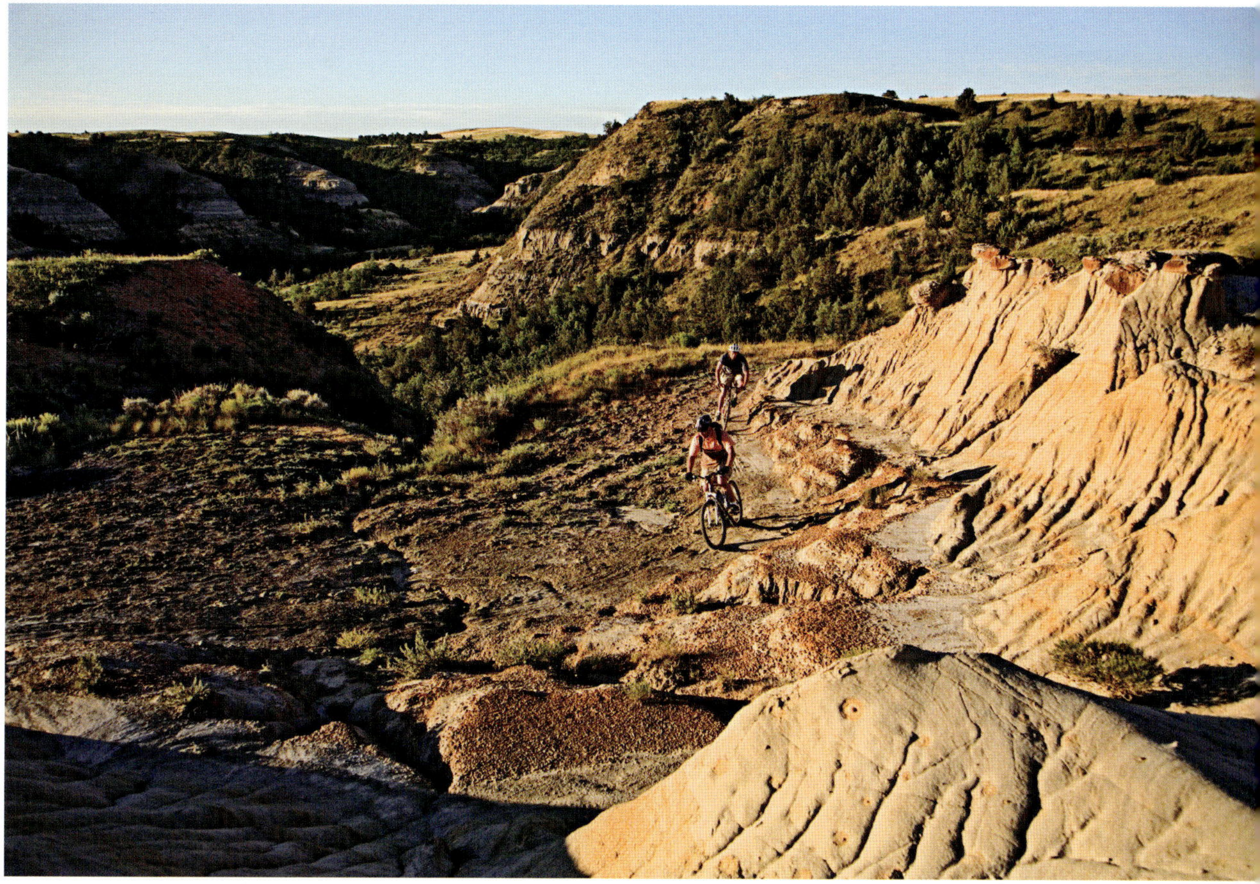

Above: Mountain bikers head down the Cottonwood Trail, part of the Maah Daah Hey Trail in the Little Missouri National Grassland. A 97-mile nonmotorized singletrack trail, the Maah Daah Hey connects all three sections of Theodore Roosevelt National Park and is one of the longest continuous singletrack mountain biking trails in the country.

Left: Golden pea or goldenbanner *(Thermopsis rhombifolia),* an early spring perennial, blooms along a trail in Theodore Roosevelt National Park. This plant is found in most western states from New Mexico north to Montana.

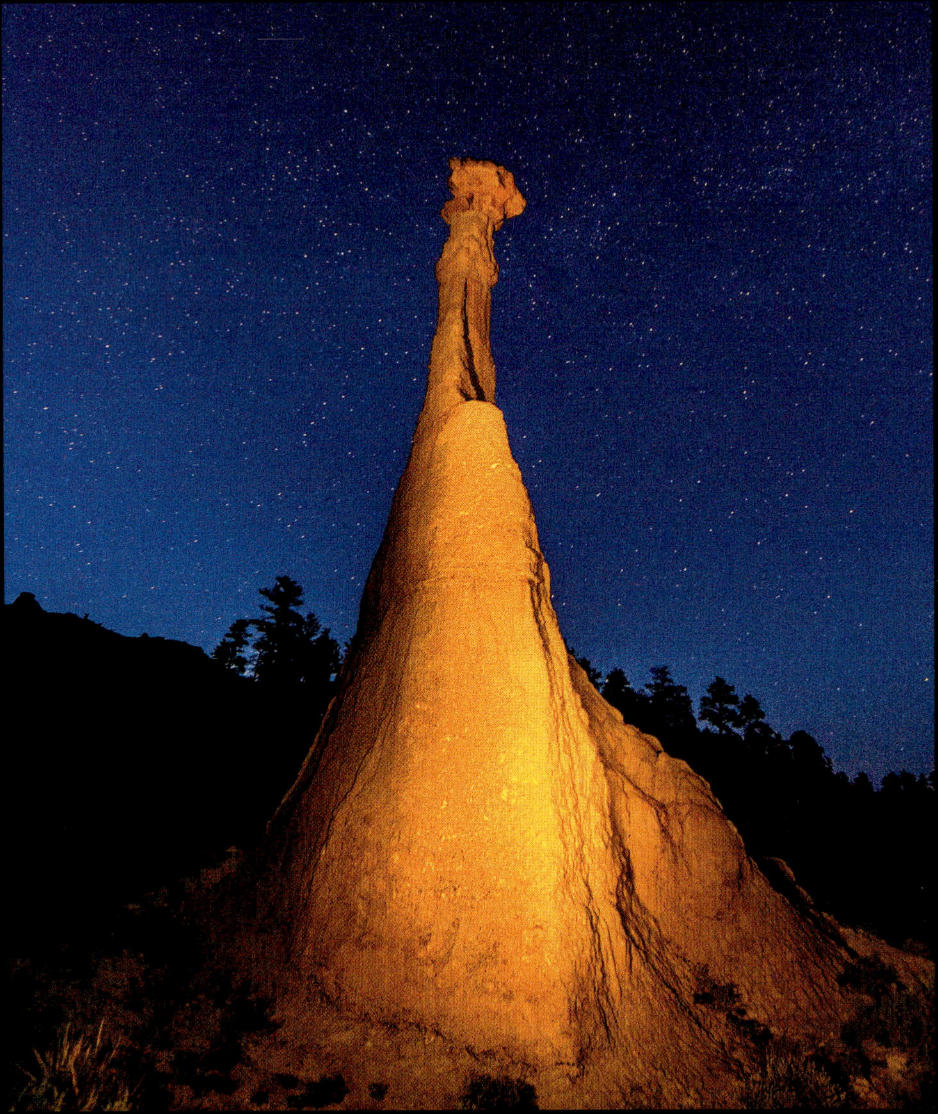

Above: One of the more distinctive caprock formations in the Upper Missouri River Breaks National Monument is lit by flashlight, with a starry night above that would have inspired Van Gogh.

Right: The Snow Creek badlands of Montana's Garfield County also feature some wonderful sandstone formations to dazzle the eye, such as this sculpted ledge near the Fort Peck Reservoir.

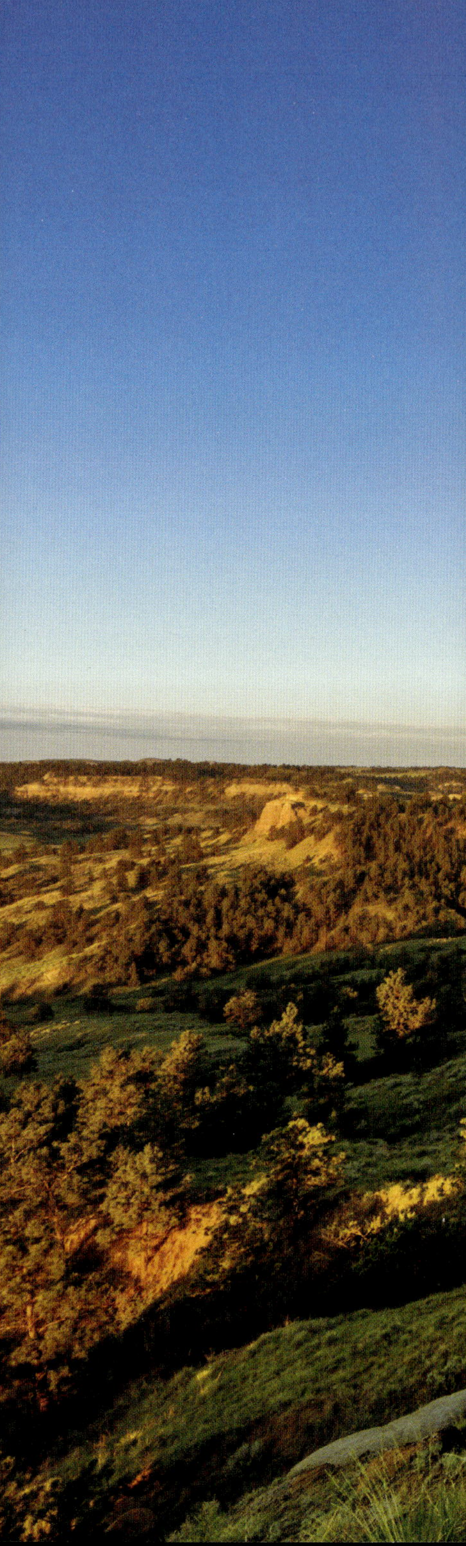

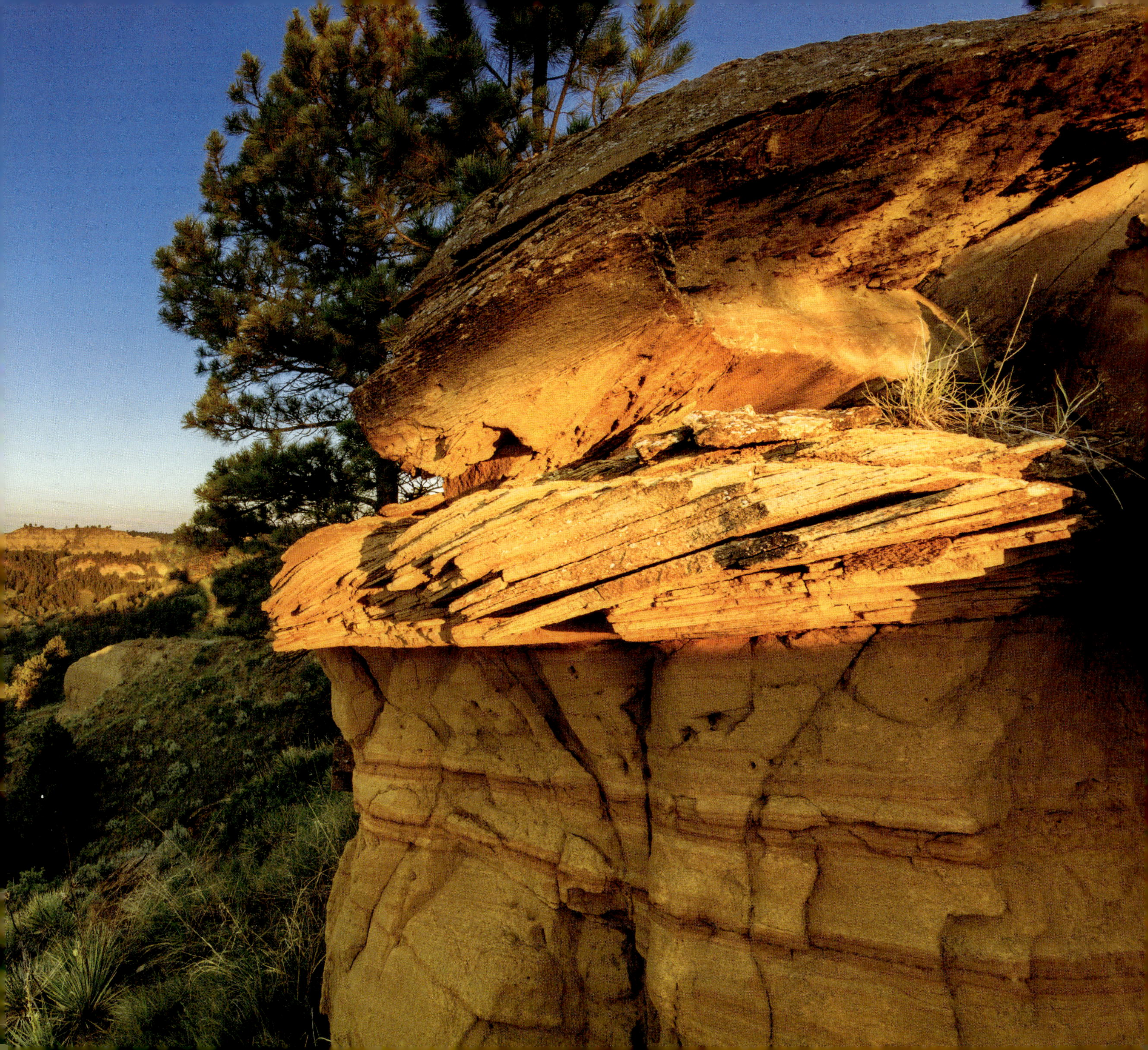

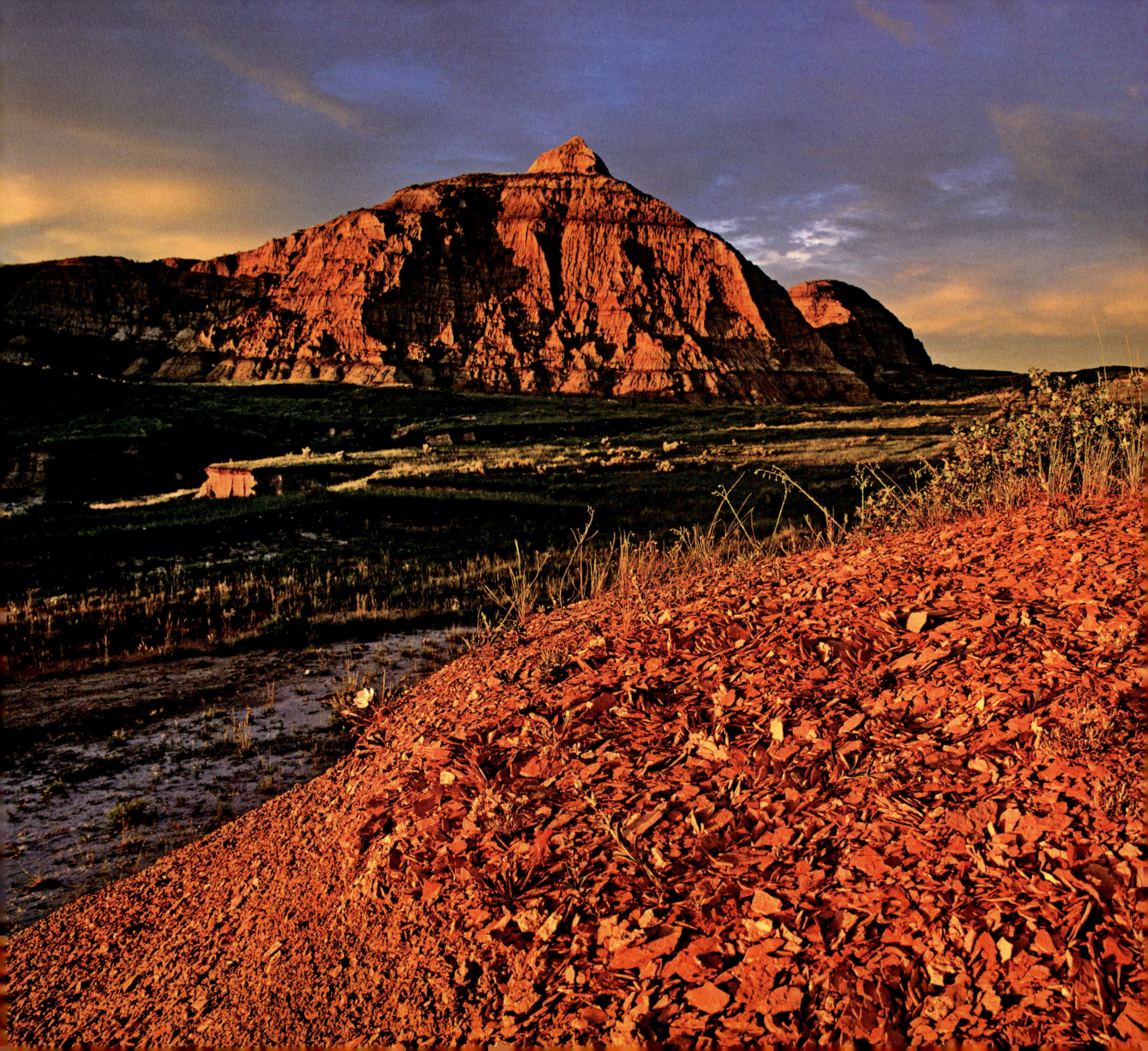

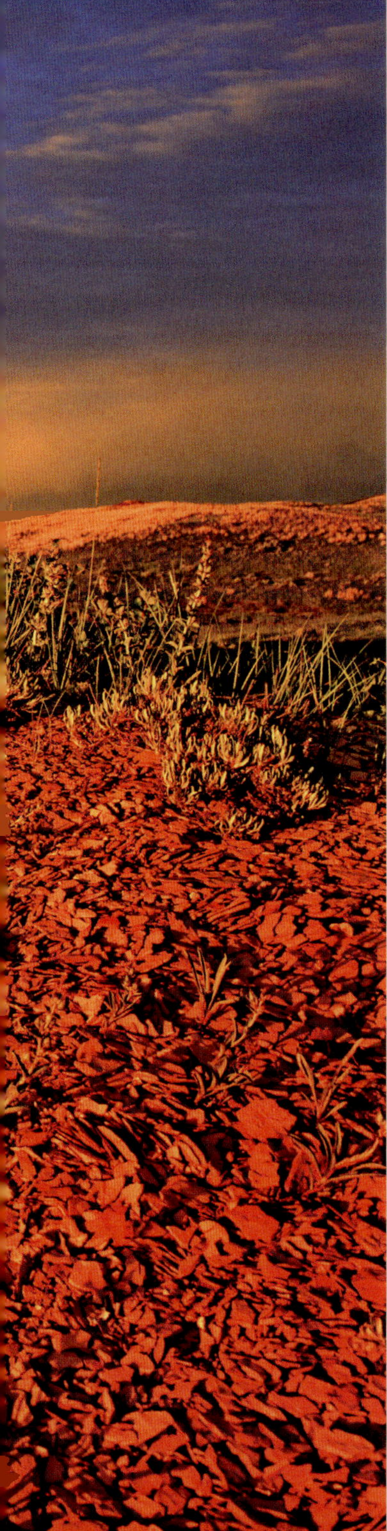

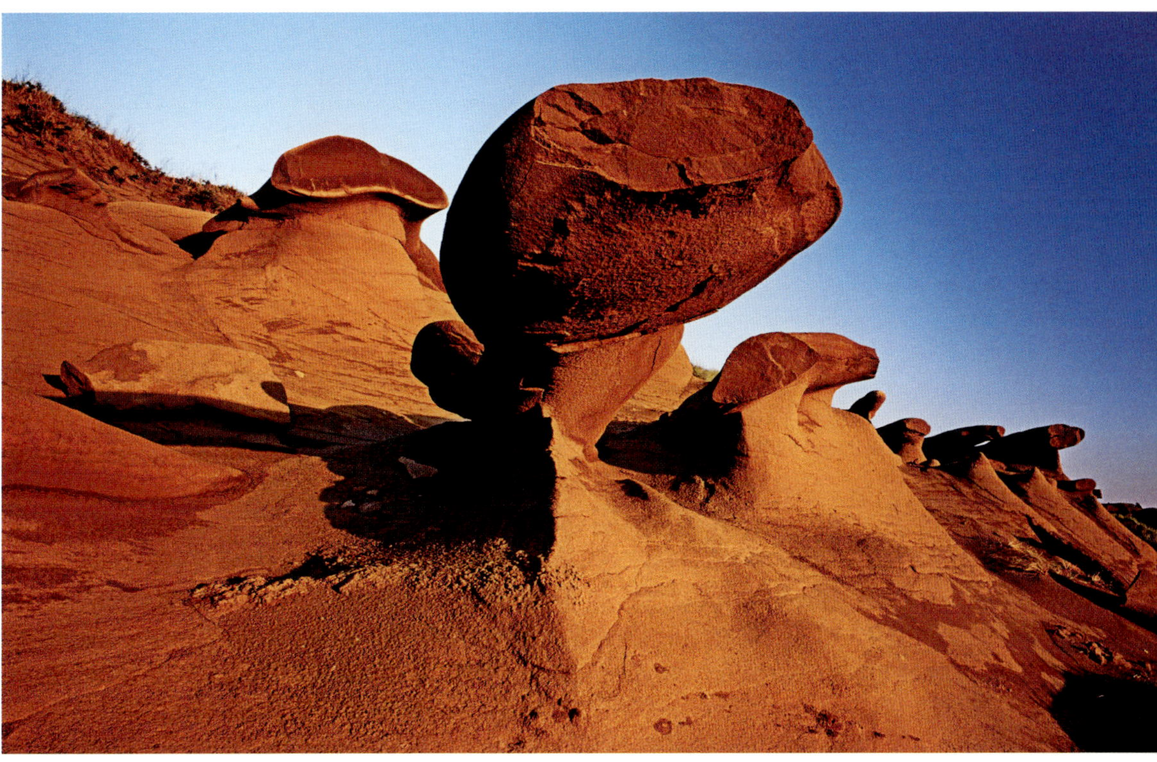

Above: These unworldly overhanging sandstone formations, found on the Sand Arroyo Badlands near Fort Peck Lake, are among the most unusual seen on badlands anywhere.

Left: Sunset light casts gorgeous colors across these badland formations in Little Missouri National Grassland. Decorating the foreground is clinker, locally called scoria, a form of baked clay.

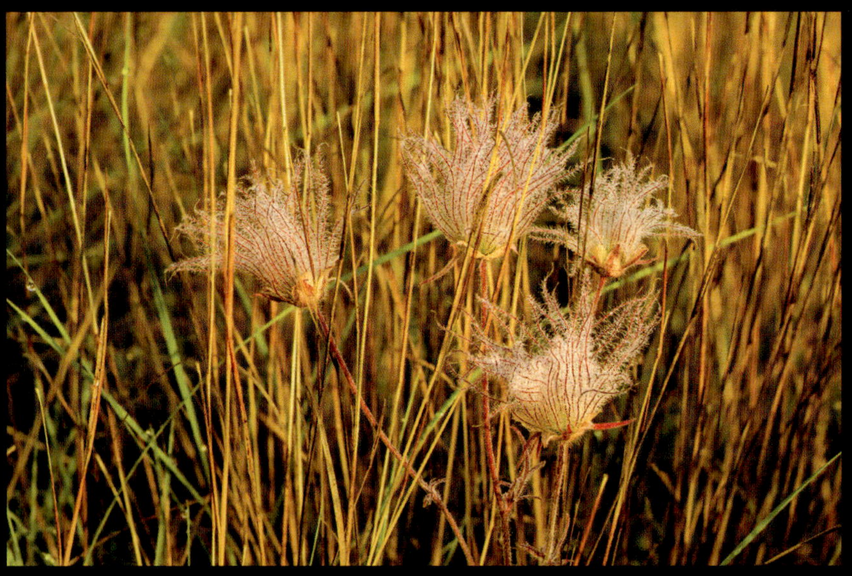

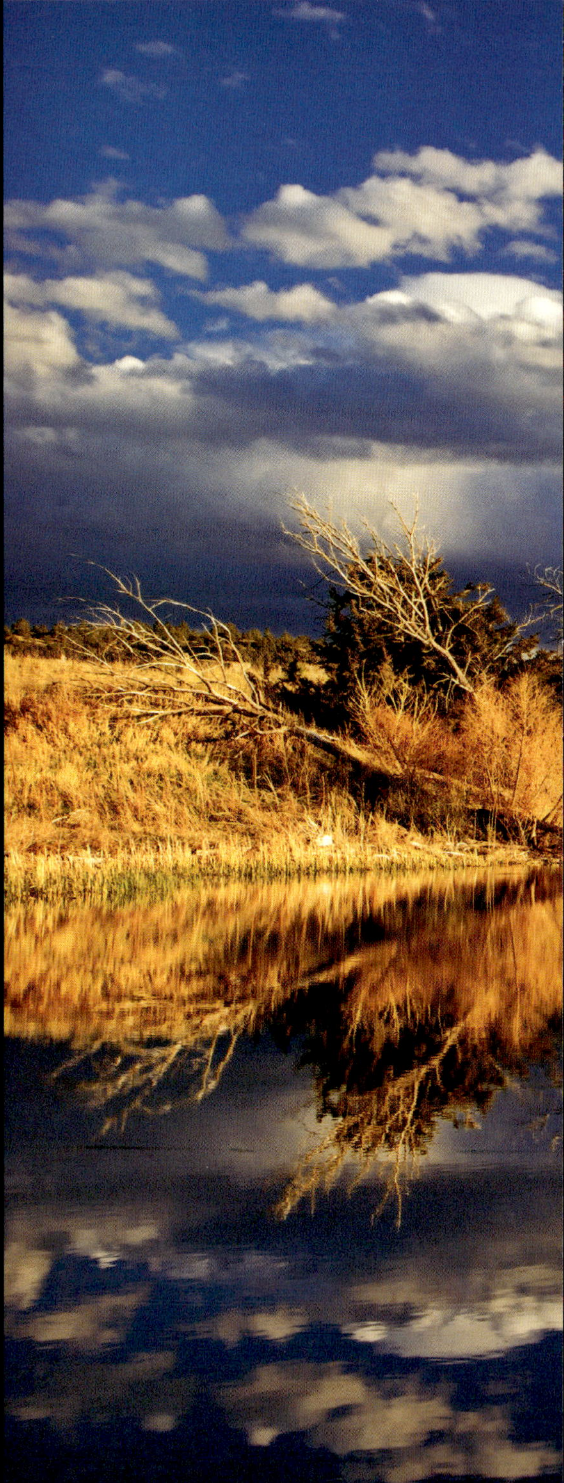

Above: In a Great Plains meadow, prairie smoke wildflowers *(Geum triflorum)* bloom in their typically feathery plumes and clusters, resembling puffs of smoke. The Blackfeet Indians boiled this plant's roots to treat a number of sores and ailments.

Right: This tranquil prairie pond reflects the hills and bluffs along with another big sky at the Buffalo Creek Wildlife Management Area near Scottsbluff, Nebraska. Part of the Wildcat Hills ecosystem and encompassing 4,300 acres, this region's wildlife include deer, elk, and turkey along with a vast array of songbirds.

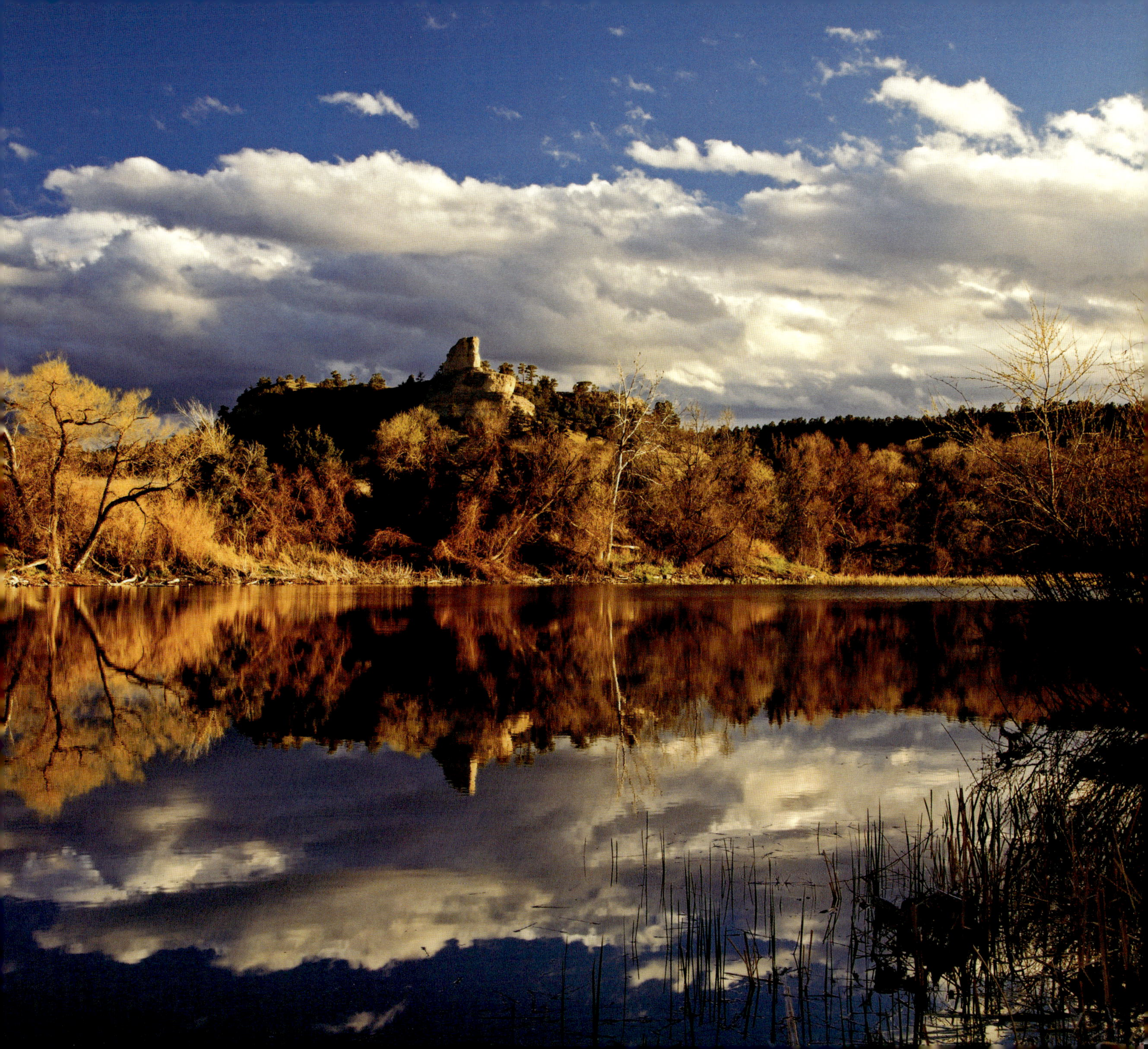

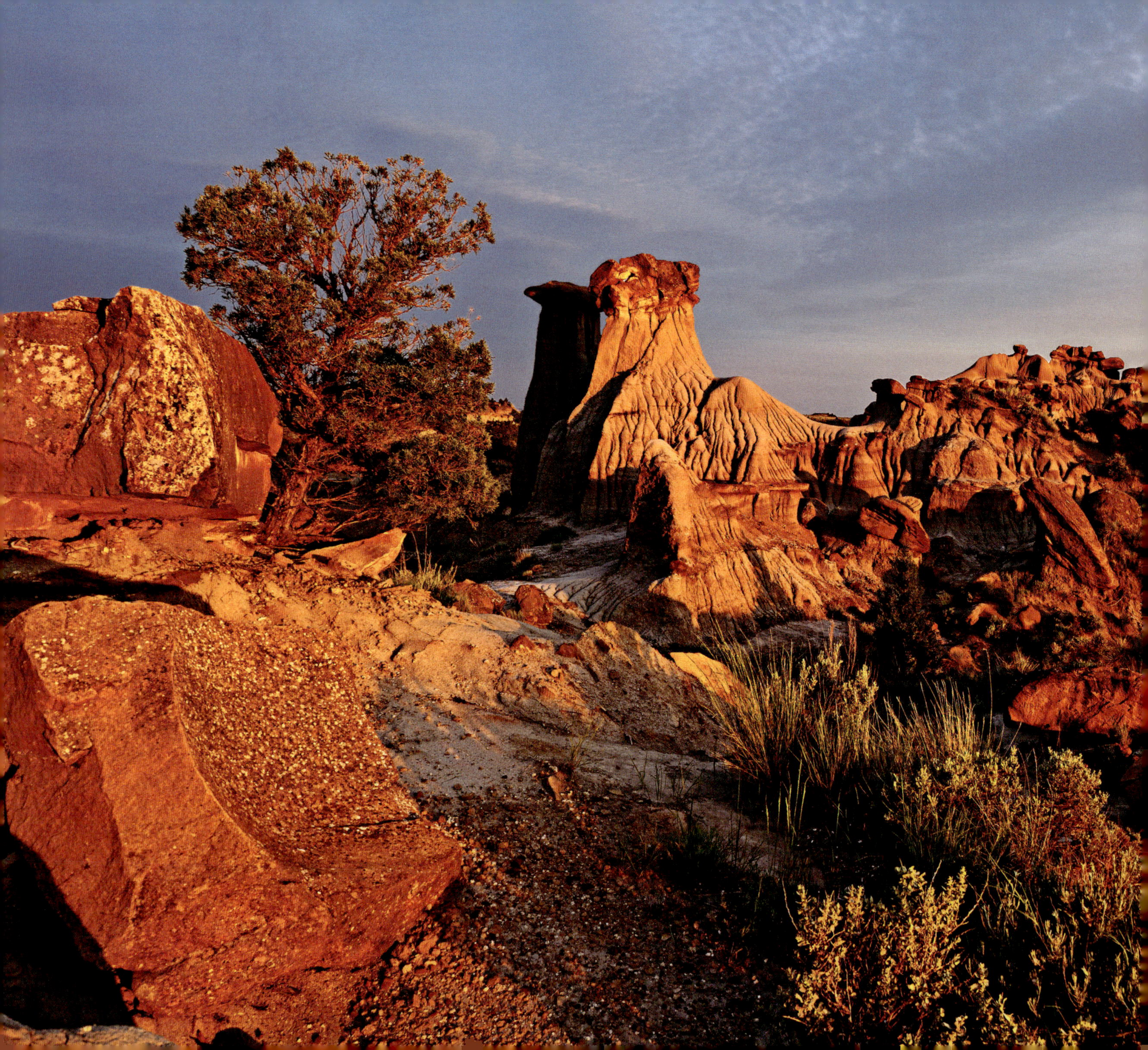

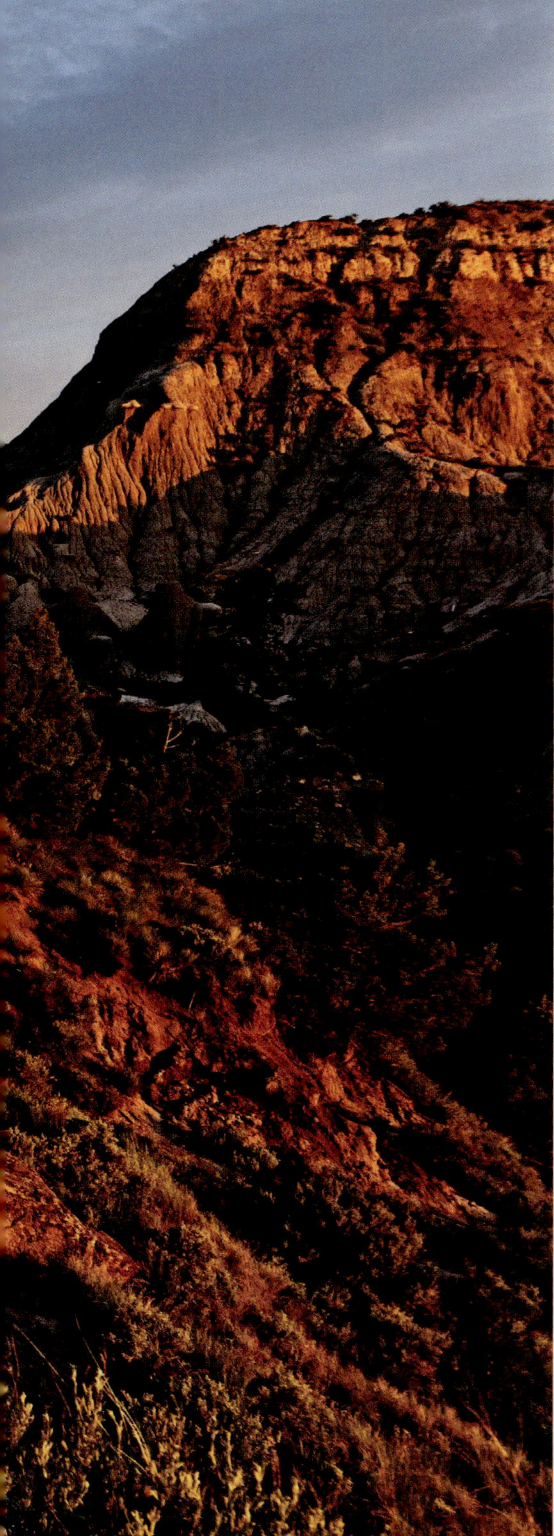

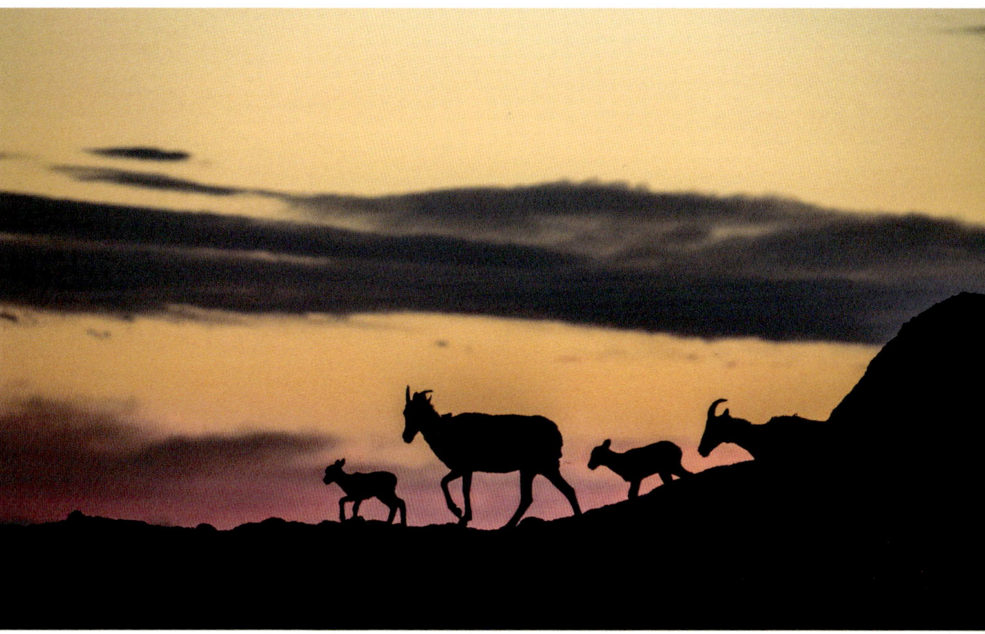

Above: Silhouetted against the light of a sunset sky in Badlands National Park, two bighorn ewes—each with a lamb—settle in for the evening. Bighorn sheep *(Ovis canadensis)* management in this park began in 1964 when 22 animals were introduced here from Pikes Peak in Colorado. The population has grown to around 75 with its health judged to be very sound.

Left: The last light of the day highlights some of the caprock formations on the badlands of Makoshika State Park near Glendive, Montana. The largest of Montana's state parks at more than 11,000 acres, this park contains many spectacular badlands landscapes like this one, which also hold abundant dinosaur fossil beds.

Right: Canoeists glide down the Missouri River past the White Cliffs at Upper Missouri River Breaks National Monument. Much of this region has remained as it was when Lewis and Clark first saw it and today is a destination spot for canoe and kayak enthusiasts from all over the world.

Below: This splendid mule deer *(Odocoileus hemionus)* buck is one of about a dozen species of mammals that roam the badlands and grasslands of Theodore Roosevelt National Park. Also among the park's fauna are at least 186 species of birds that include golden eagles, sharp-tailed grouse, and wild turkeys.

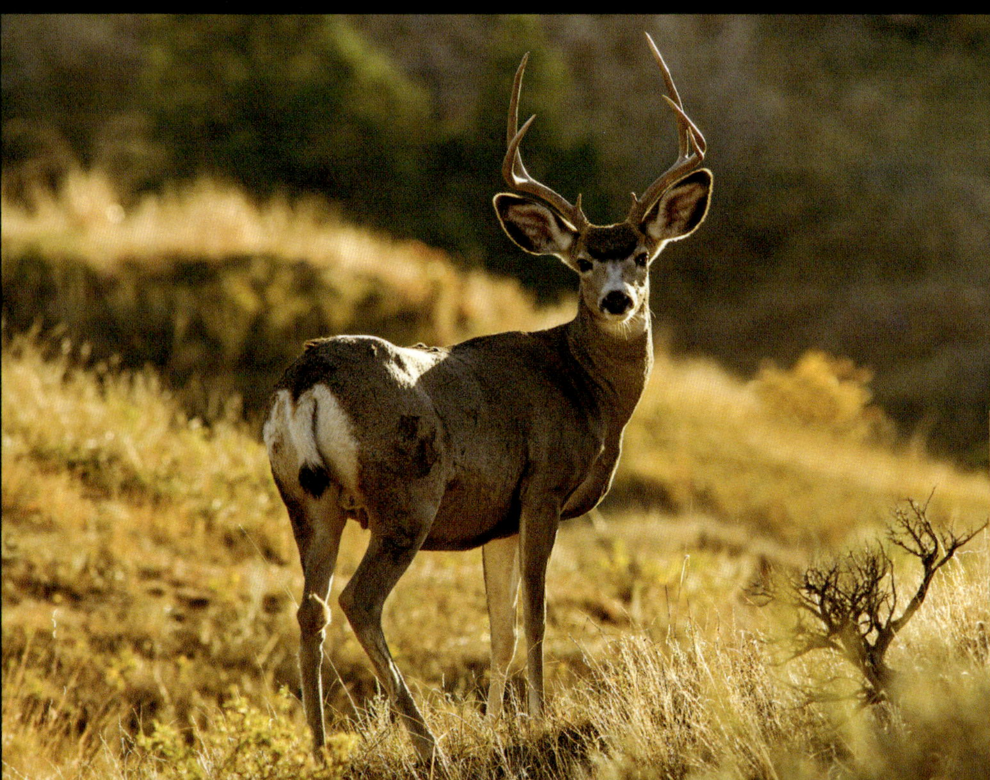

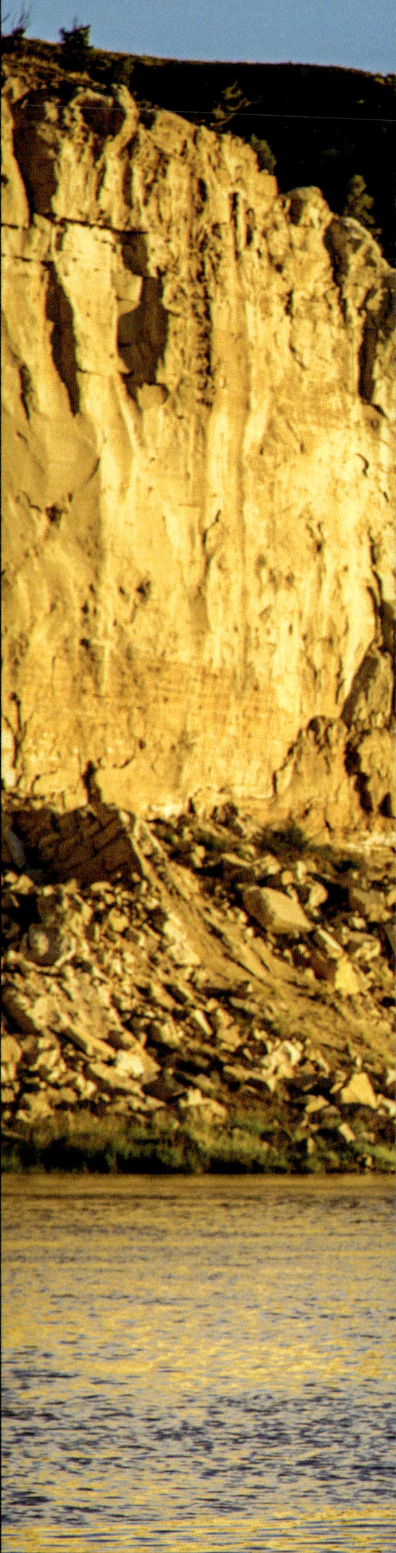

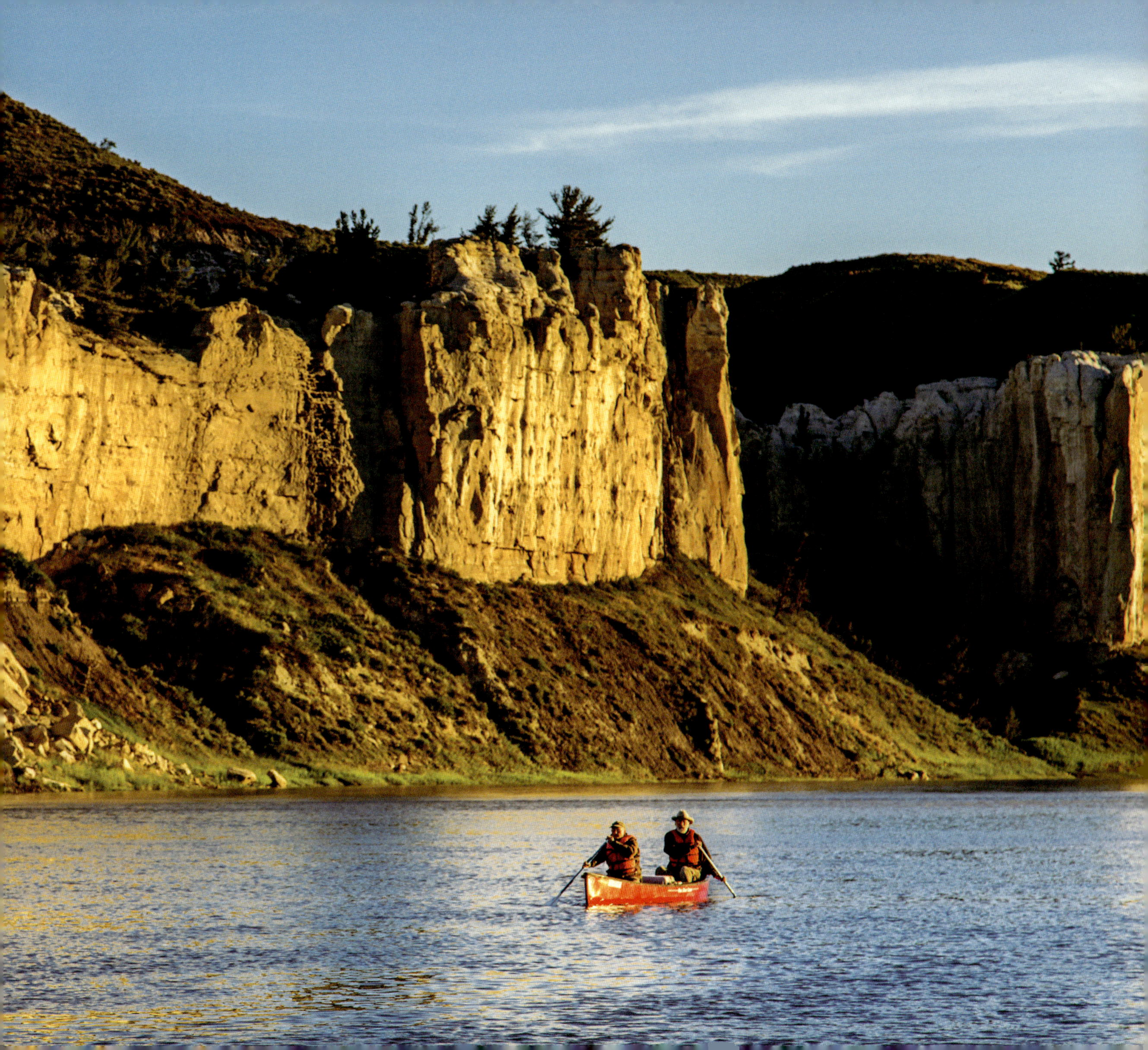

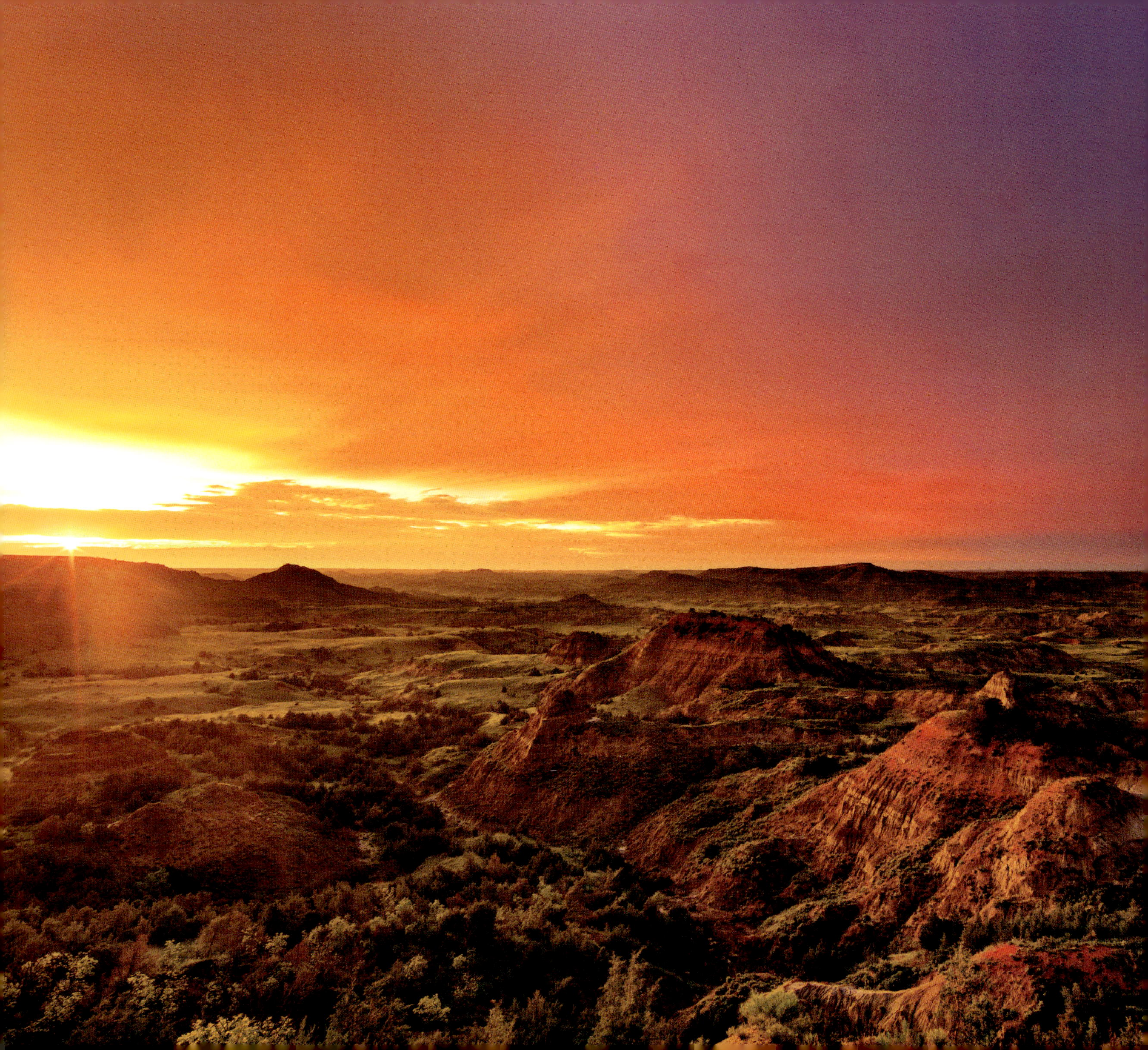

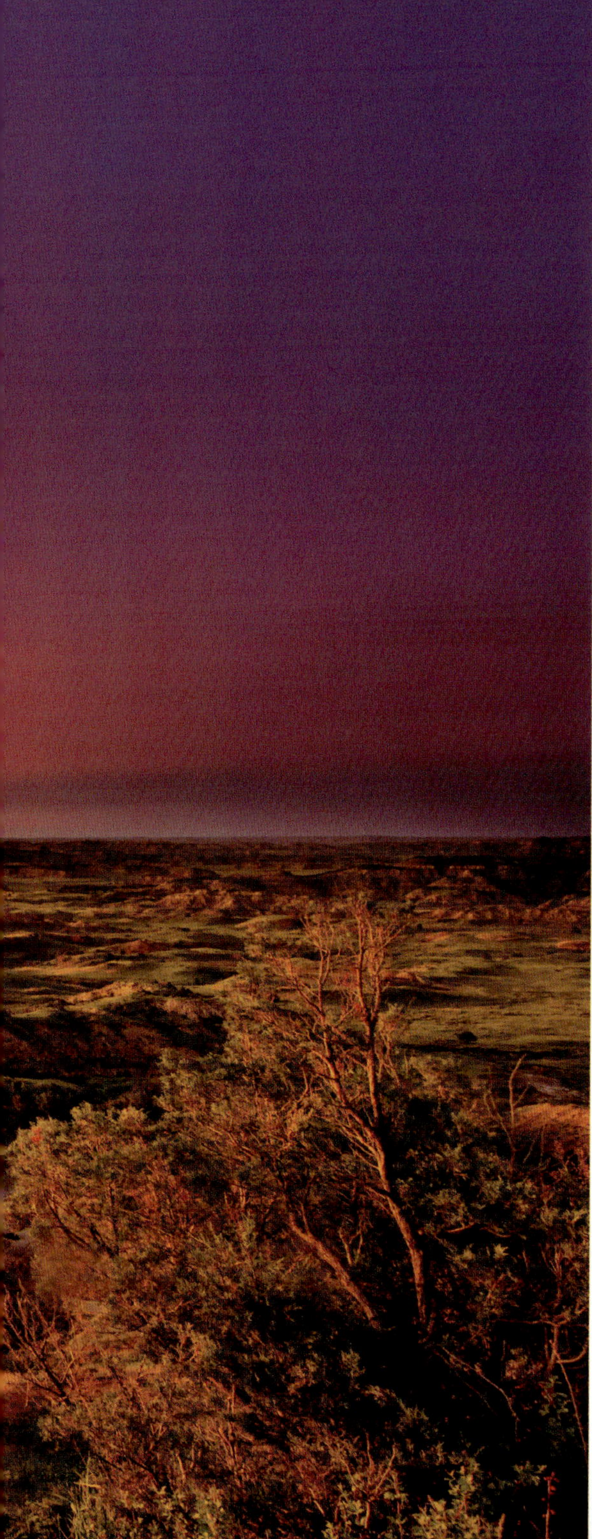

Left: An evening thunderstorm appears over Theodore Roosevelt National Park's Painted Canyon, one of the park's most popular attractions. The scenery here undergoes constant changes in relationship to the seasons. While brown and dormant grass is dominant from late summer through winter, early summer explodes with green color and hundreds of flowering plants.

Below: Fossilized leaves are inscribed in this sandstone ridge at North Dakota's Fort Stevenson State Park on Lake Sakakawea's north shore. This park has more than eight miles of nonmotorized trails for hiking, biking, and cross-country skiing. A half-mile trail winds through the park's new arboretum, which contains fifty native and nonnative trees, shrubs, wildflowers, and grasses.

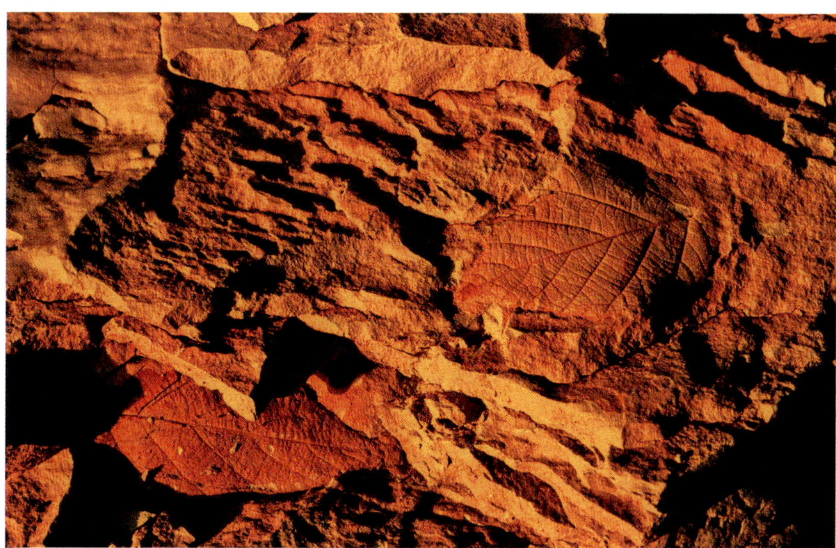

Right: Sentinel Rock in the Scotts Bluff National Monument glows in the light of a gathering storm in western Nebraska. The monument consists of five rock formations: Crown Rock, Dome Rock, Eagle Rock, Saddle Rock, and Sentinel Rock.

Below: A combination of wind and water erosion over various geologic epochs has carved bizarre land surfaces like this one lit by the light of a waning day on Little Missouri National Grassland.

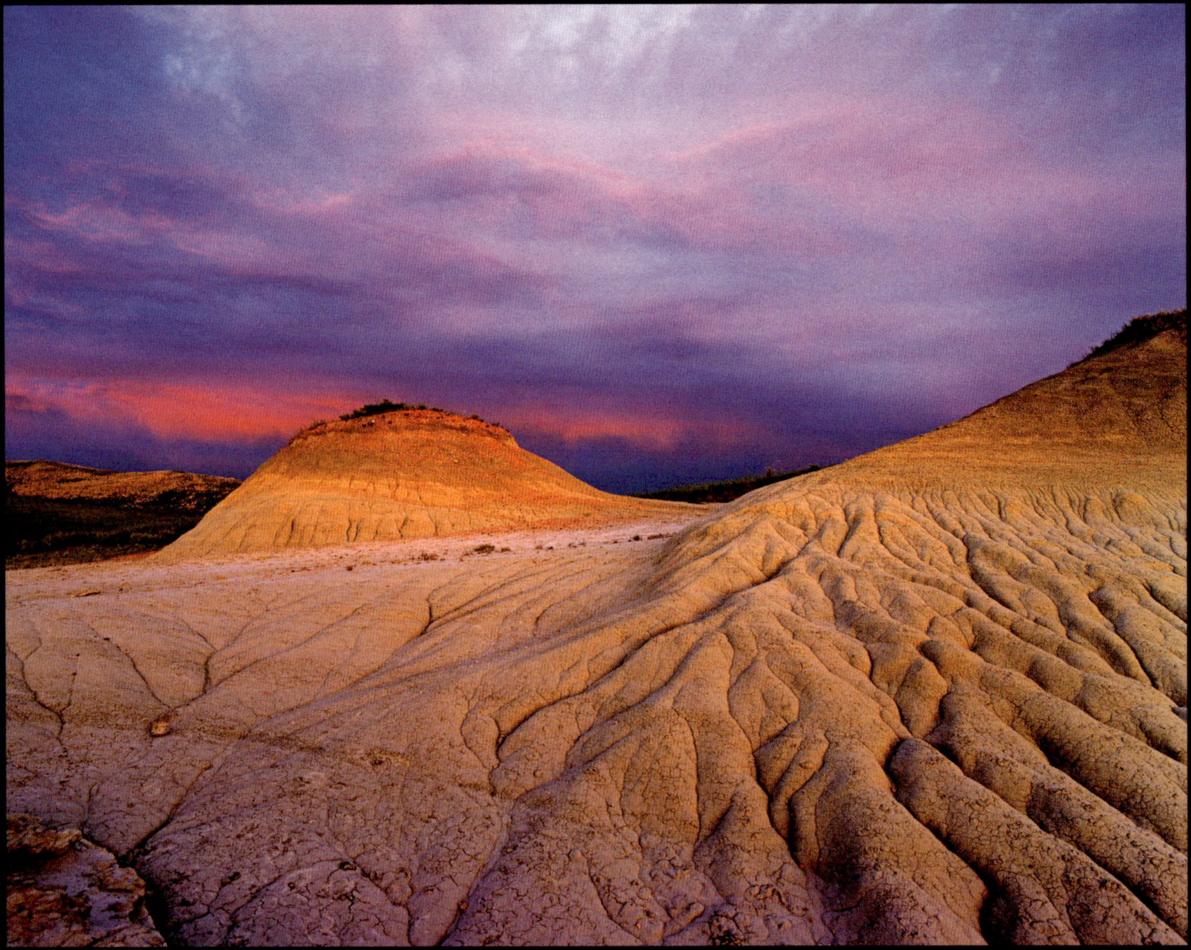

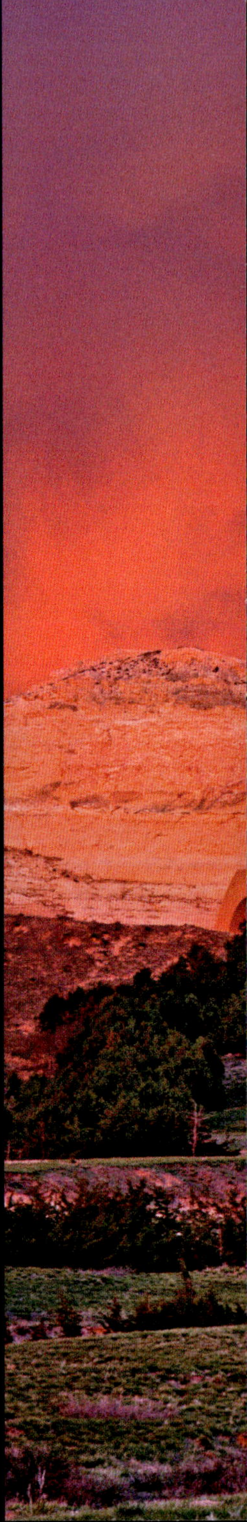

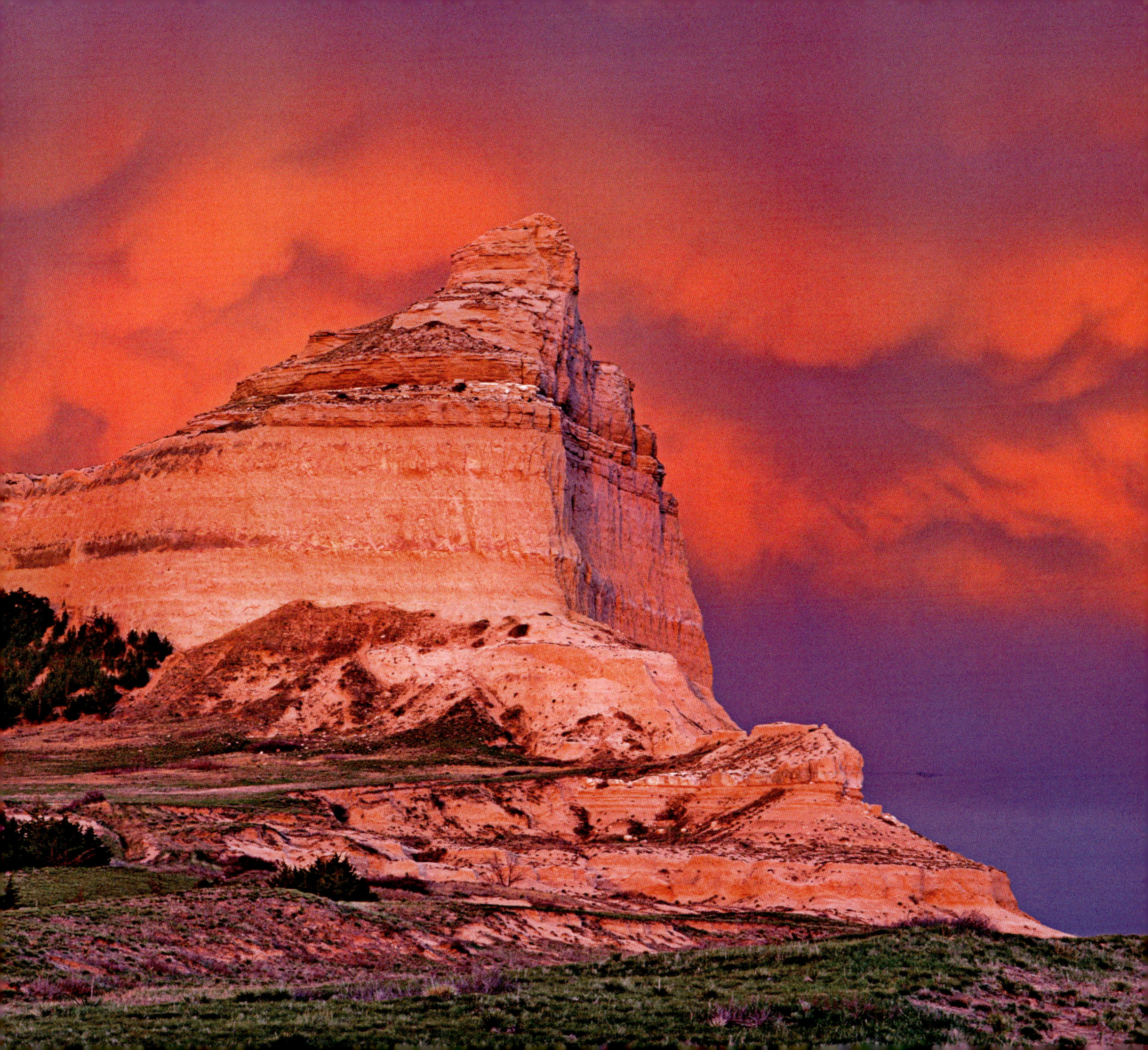

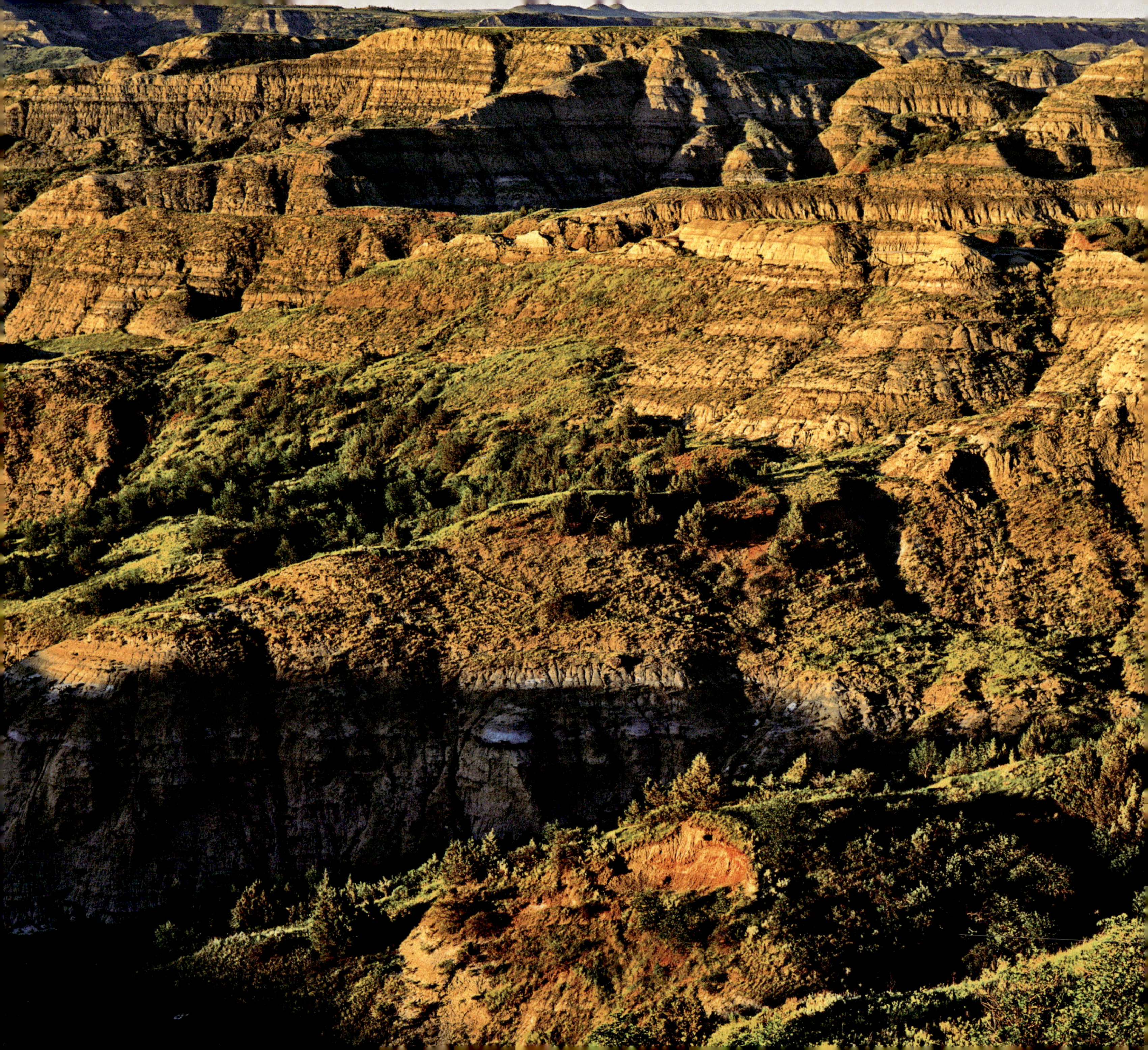

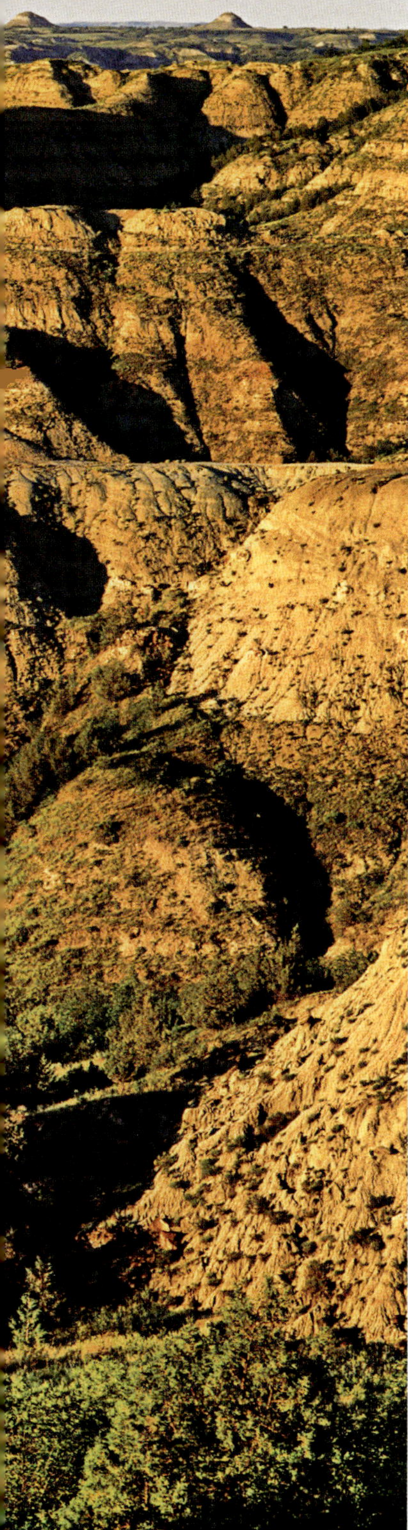

Left: Some of the most rugged and striking badlands landscapes found anywhere are in North Dakota's Little Missouri State Park near Killdeer. Much of this primitive park is not accessible by car, only by horse and on foot. There are 47 miles of trails with horse corrals available for those bringing in their own horses and artesian wells within the park for watering horses.

Below: No more than a few days old, this pronghorn *(Antilocapra americana)* fawn waits for its mother, one of these does, to lead it to another hiding place in the grasslands of Custer State Park in South Dakota. This little one will spend most of its first month in hiding, eluding predators like the clever coyote. About 50,000 of these fabled creatures roam the prairies of western South Dakota.

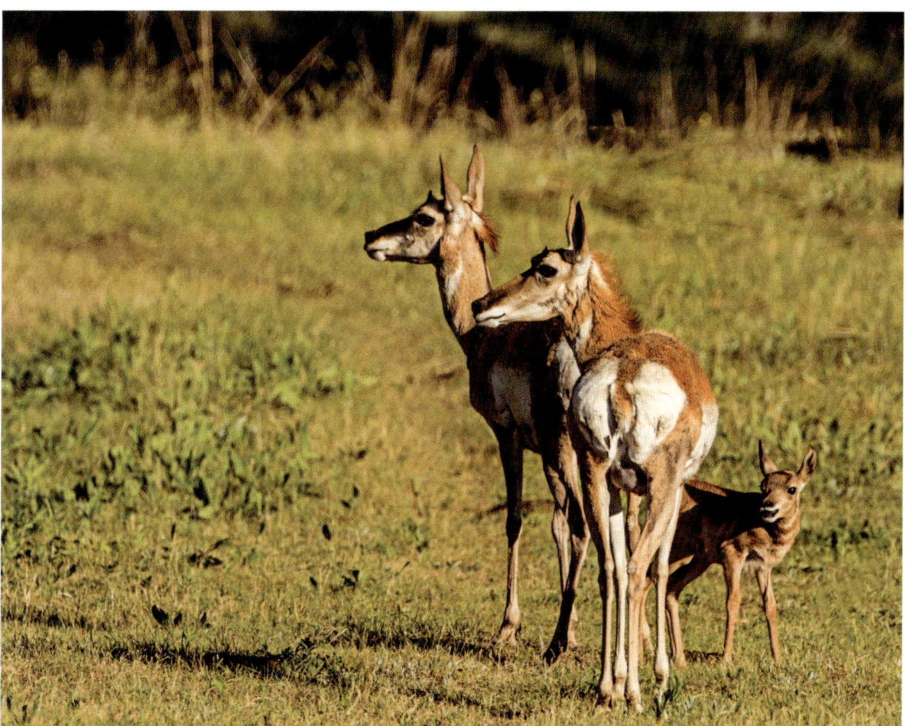

Right: This caprock formation highlights the badlands landscape at Upper Missouri River Breaks National Monument. The Breaks are home to at least 60 mammal species and hundreds of bird species. Willows and shrubs grow along the Missouri River banks with sage brush and short-grass prairie being dominant elsewhere.

Below: Bighorn sheep lambs forage in the grasslands of an upper plateau area just off Sage Creek Rim Road in the northern section of Badlands National Park. This park is home to at least thirty-nine mammals that include these Rocky Mountain bighorn sheep, bison, badgers, bobcats, coyotes, deer, pronghorn, and the reintroduced black-footed ferret, North America's most endangered land mammal.

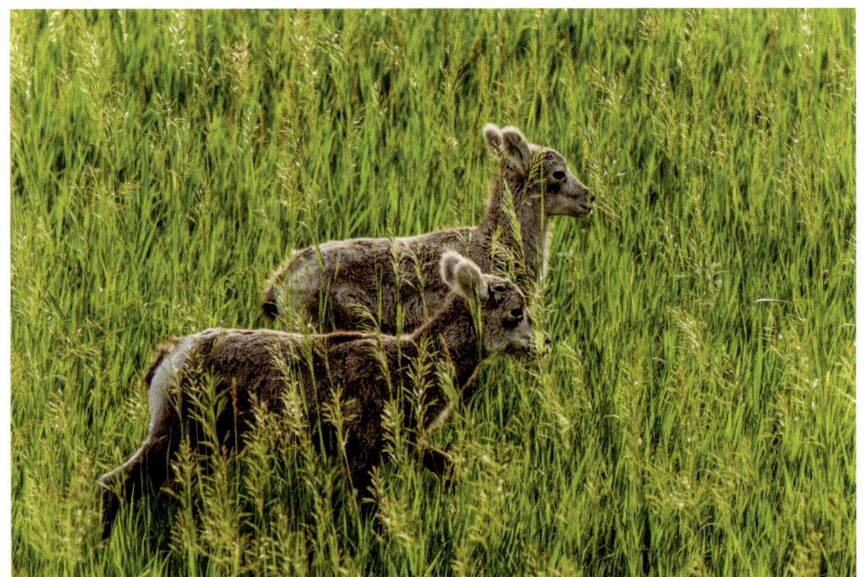

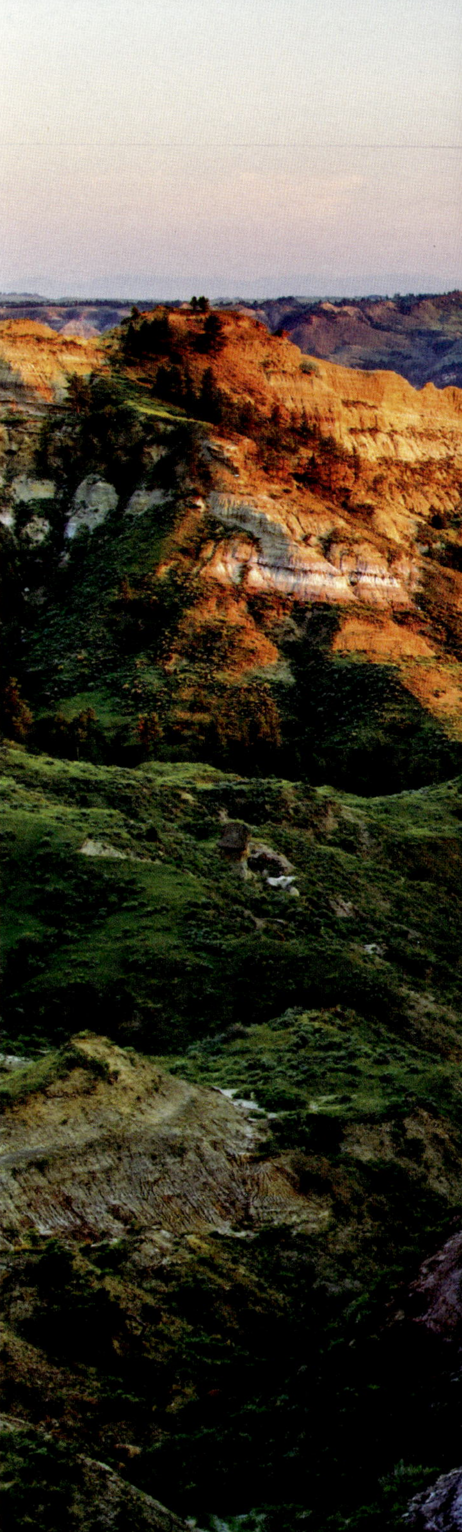

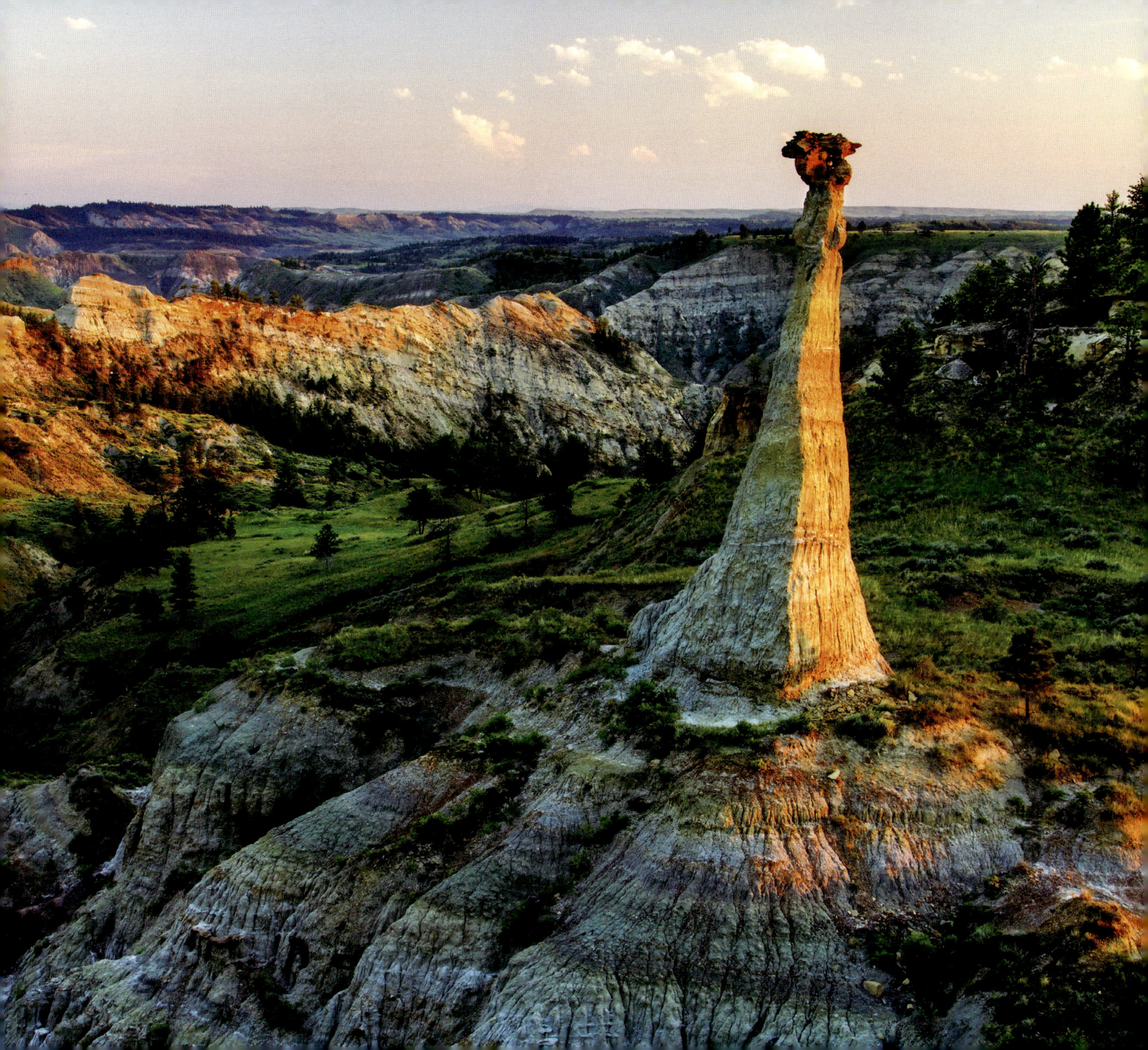

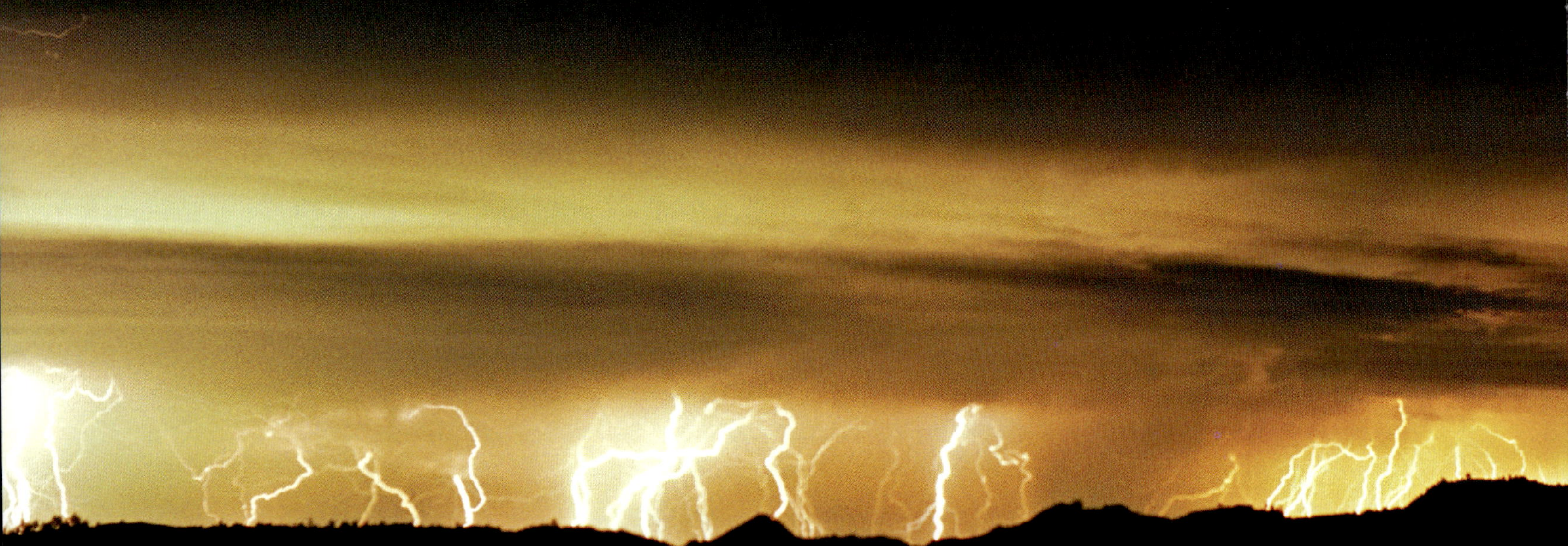

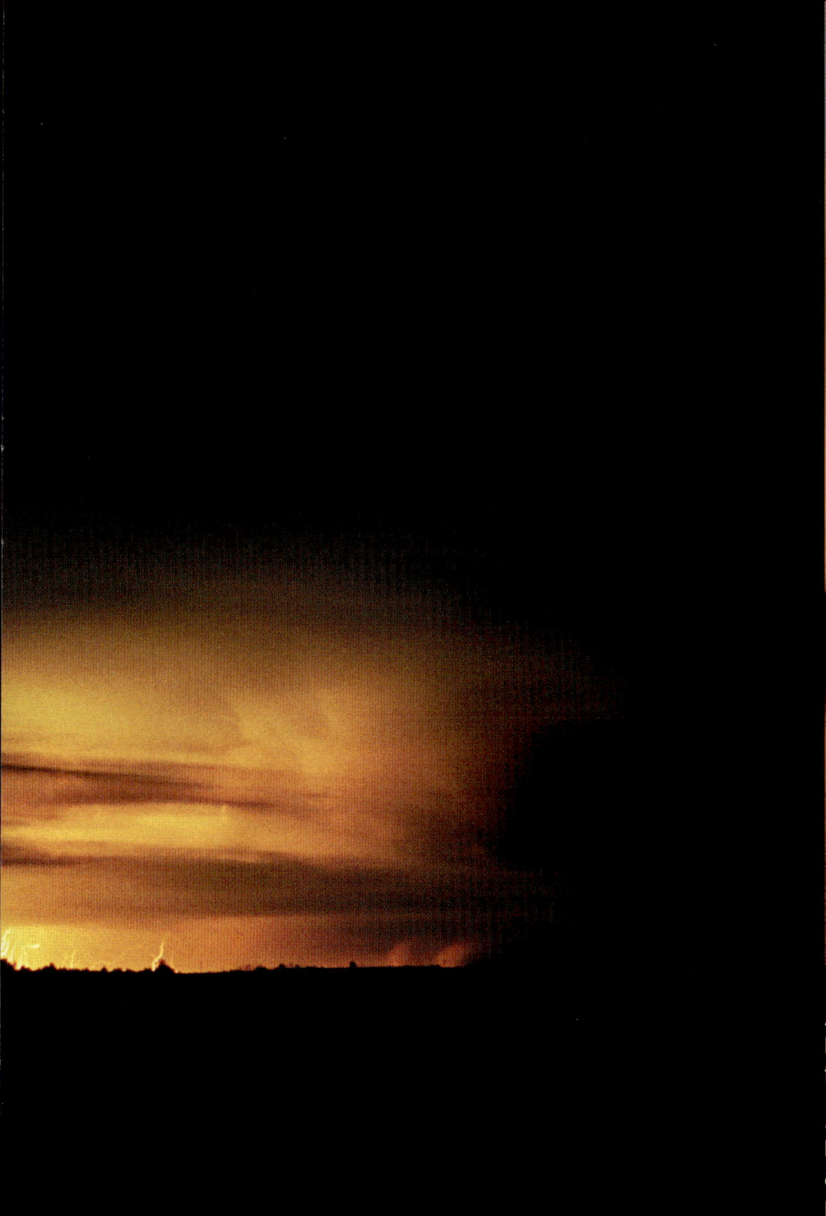

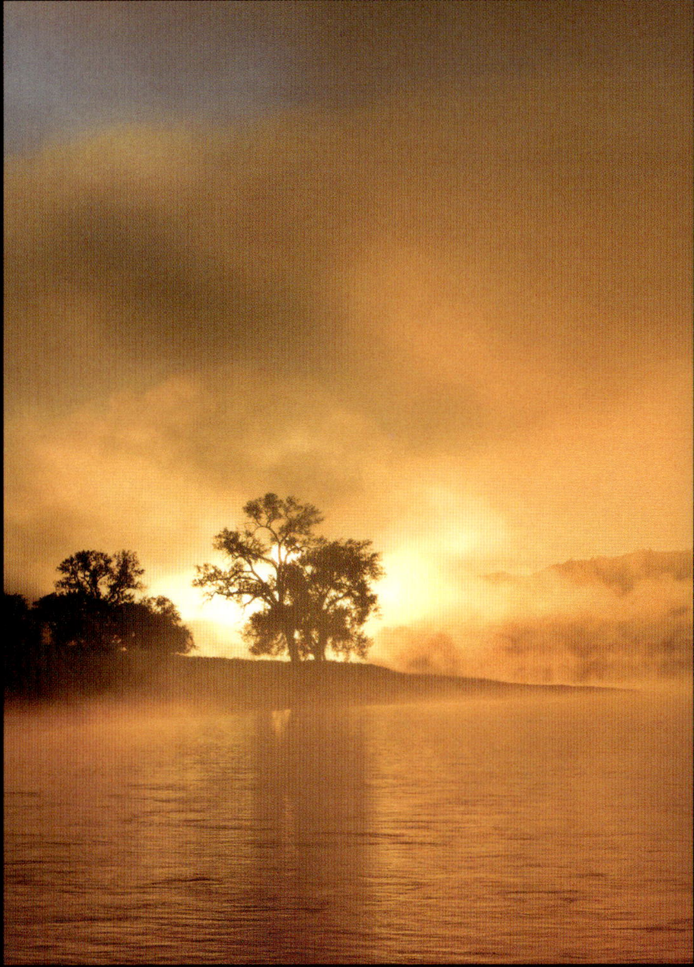

Above: Sunrise breaks through a heavy fog on the Missouri River at Upper Missouri River Breaks National Monument. Forty-nine species of fish reside in the river and its tributaries here that include walleye, catfish, and northern pike.

Left: An intense display of lightning commands the skies over Makoshika State Park during an early evening thunderstorm. A distinct lack of light "pollution" across much of the Great Plains—due to fewer major metropolitan areas—provides various opportunities for spectacular nighttime photography.

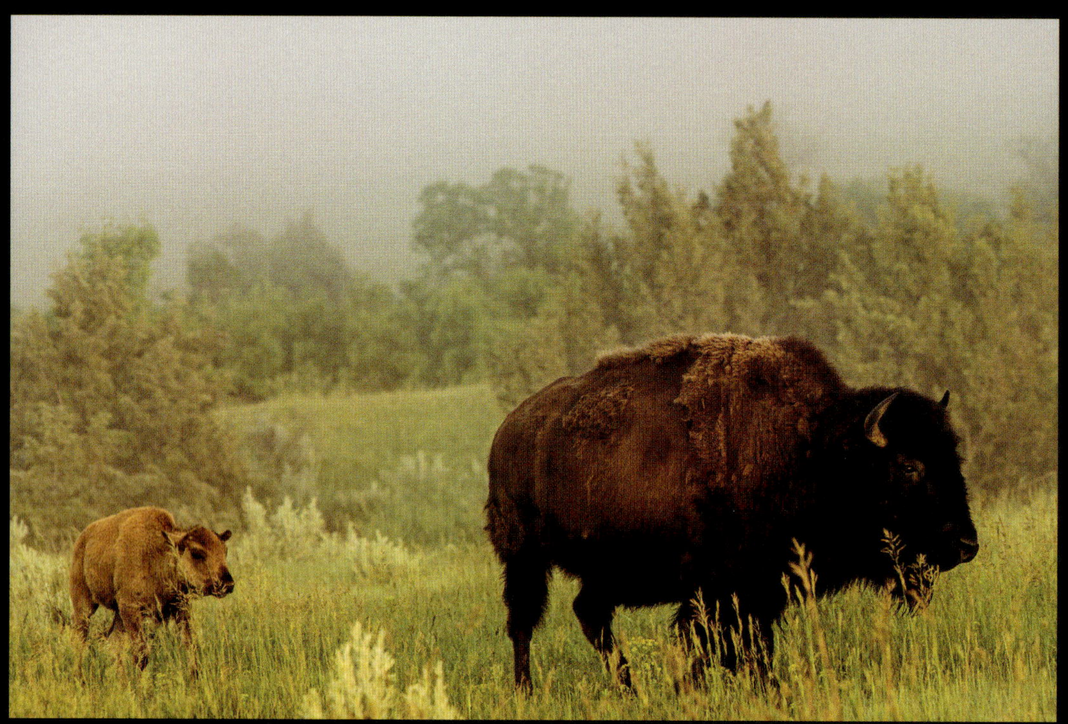

Above A month-old bison calf follows along behind its mother through a forested ravine on the prairie. About sixty pounds at birth, bison calves are born with this golden brown coat that has usually turned to the adult's chocolate brown by three months of age.

Right: This meadow in Badlands National Park is filled with one of the region's most prolific mid summer perennials, the upright prairie coneflower *(Rudbeckia laciniata)*. The striking yellow blossoms of this plant were used by Native Americans to make dyes.

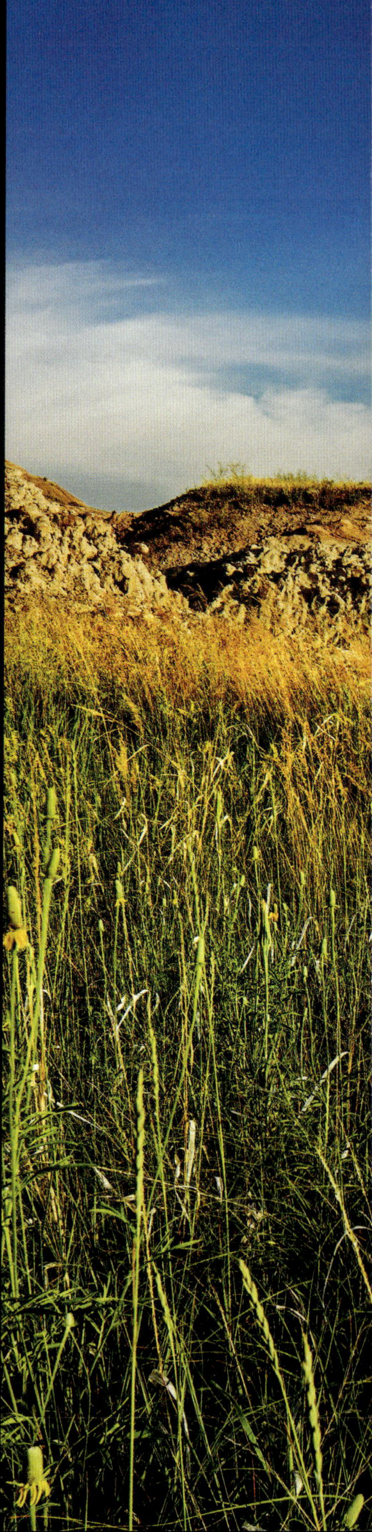

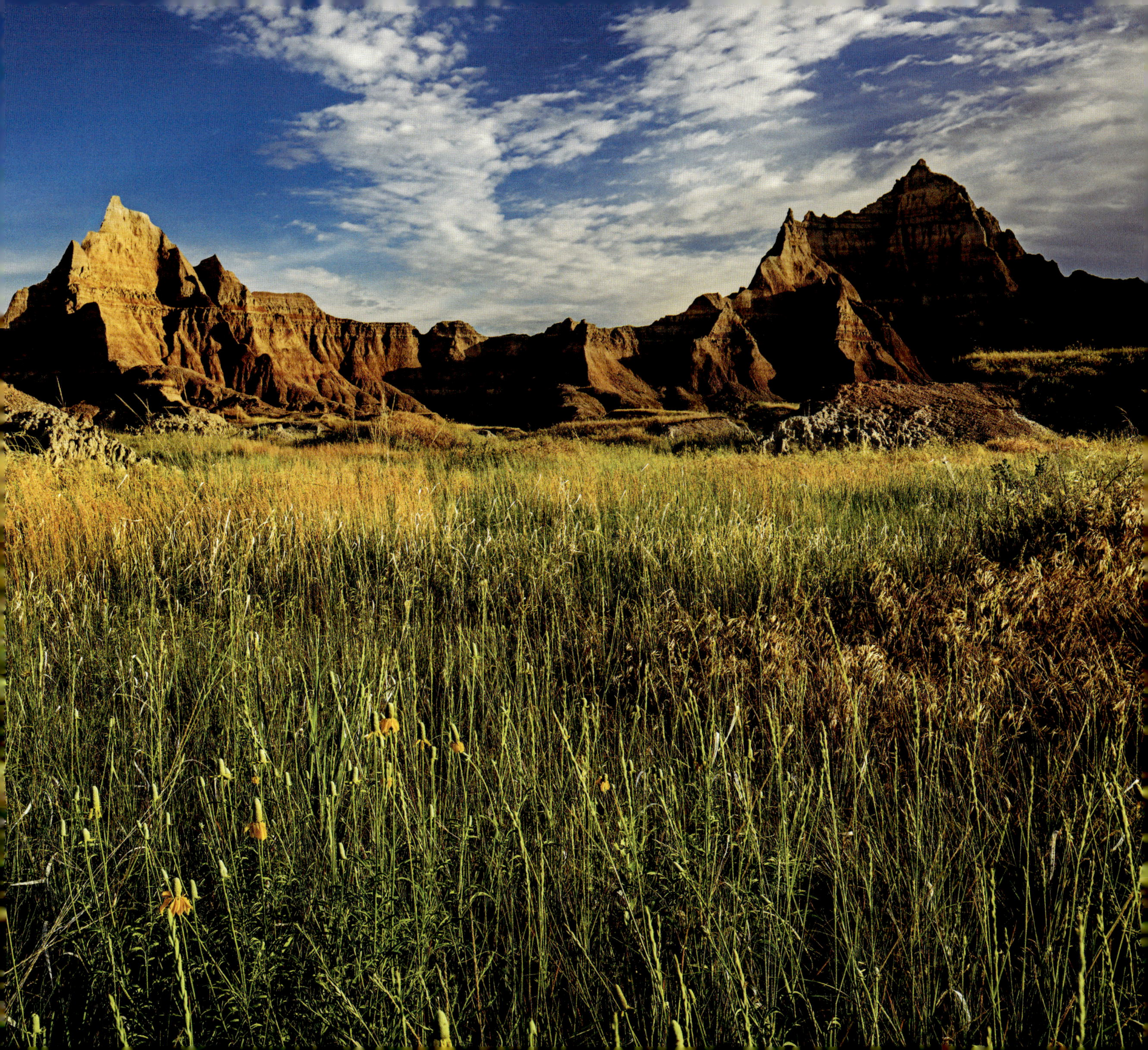

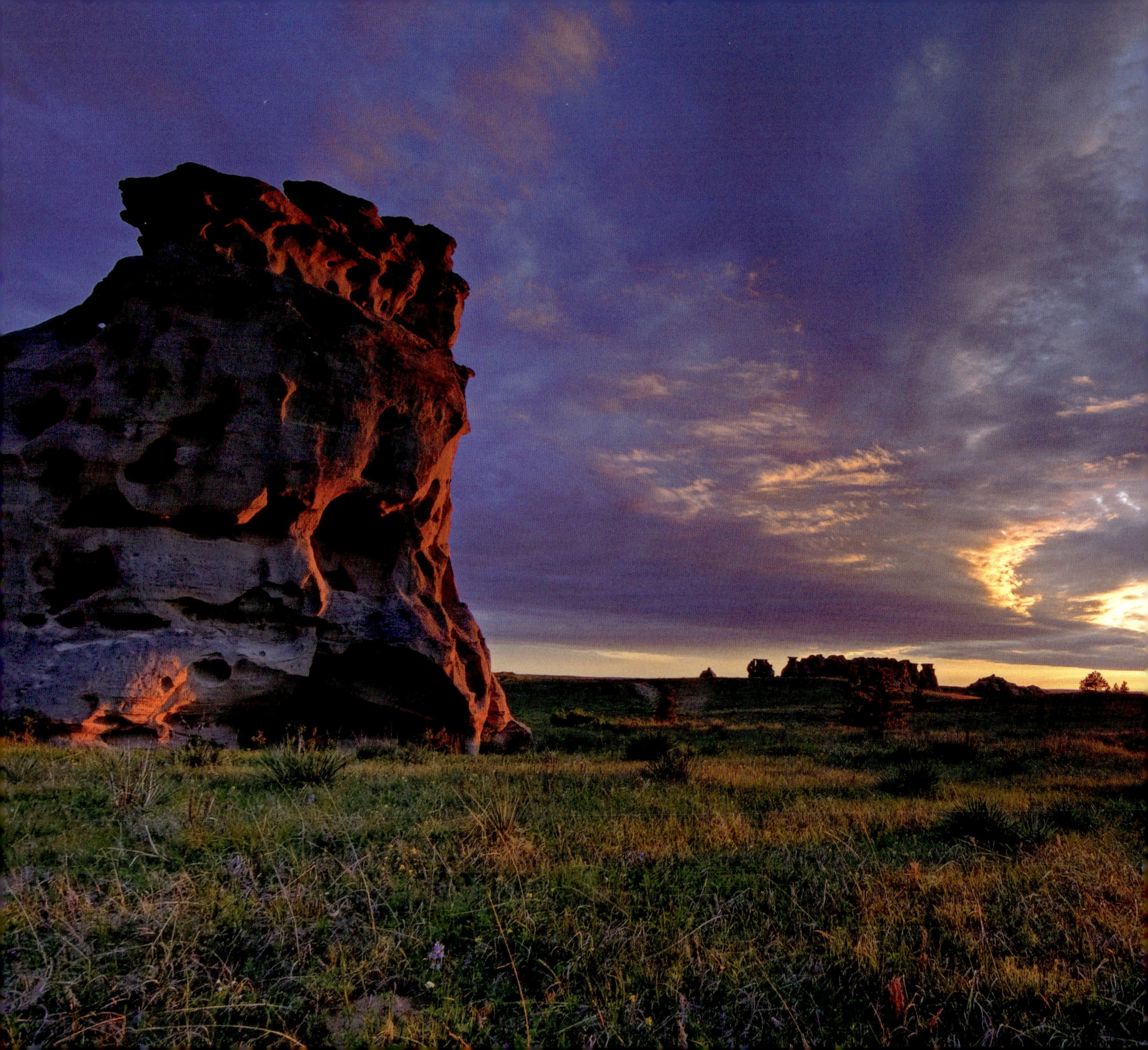

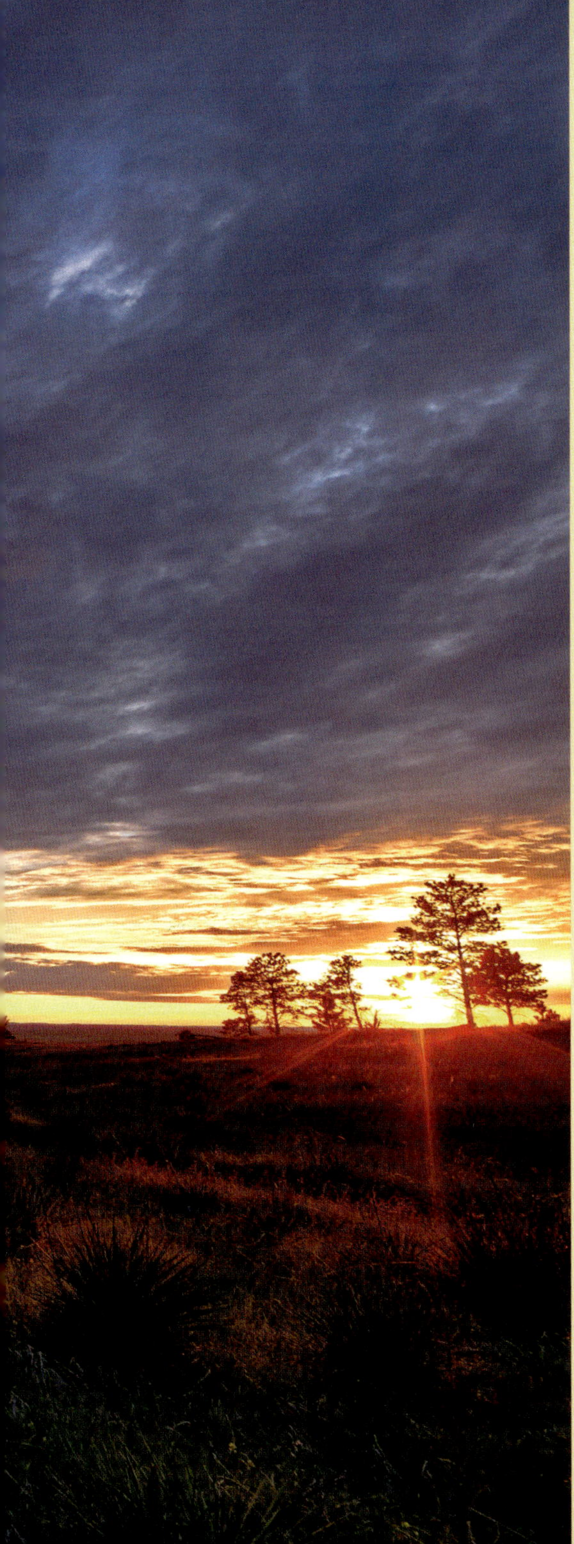

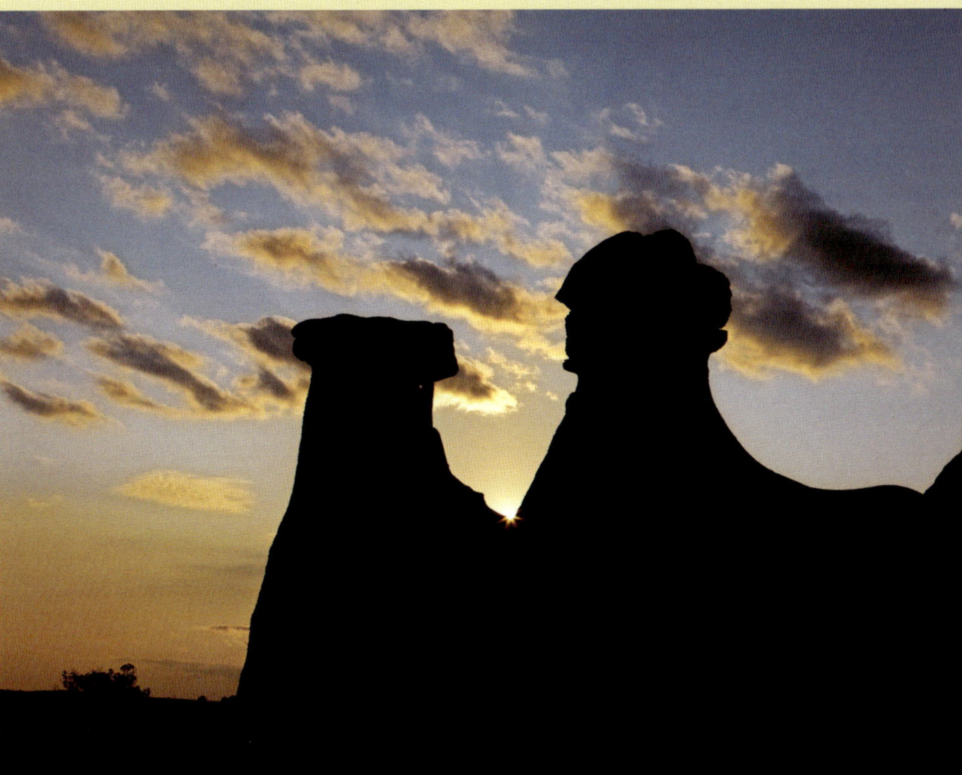

Above: Silhouetted against a fading prairie sky, these caprock formations at Makoshika State Park provide perches and nesting sites for raptor birds like the turkey vulture, prairie falcon, and golden eagle. Makoshika comes from the Lakota words *Maco sica* which means bad land or land of bad spirits.

Left: One of the trademarks of a Great Plains landscape is always the huge sky resplendent with cloud-filled color, especially at sunset. A Swiss cheese rock formation is framed beneath one of those skies in Medicine Rocks State Park.

Right: From its perch atop sagebrush in Montana's Garfield County, the "prairie's orator", a western meadowlark *(Sturnella neglecta)* sings its lovely flute-like song across the grasslands. Many people of the prairie consider the opening day of spring to be the first day they hear the meadowlark's song after its long winter absence.

Far right: A dramatic storm front and clouds form at sunrise over Badlands National Park near Wall. These badlands took forty-seven million years to form, spanning three major geologic periods—the Cretaceous period and the Late Eocene and Oligocene epochs.

Below: Mid-June can be a spectacular time in the badlands with sprawling meadows of color from blooming succulents like this prickly pear cactus *(Opuntia polyacantha)* and many other midsummer perennials.

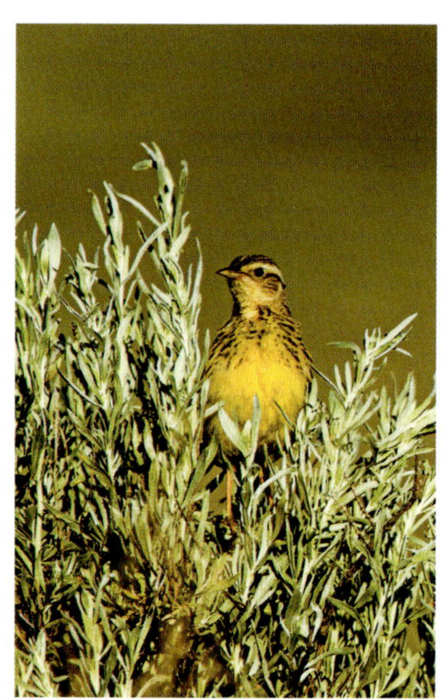

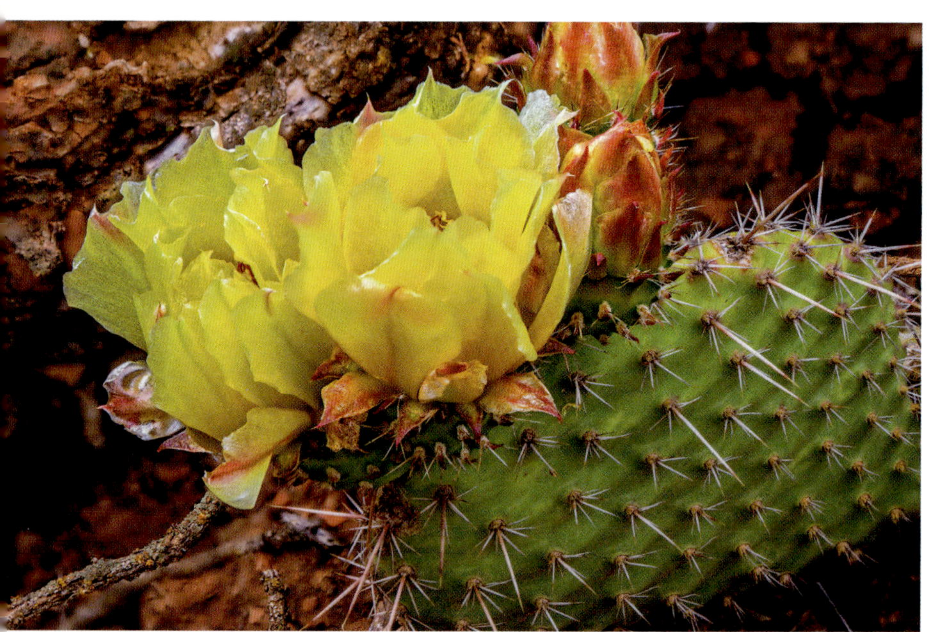

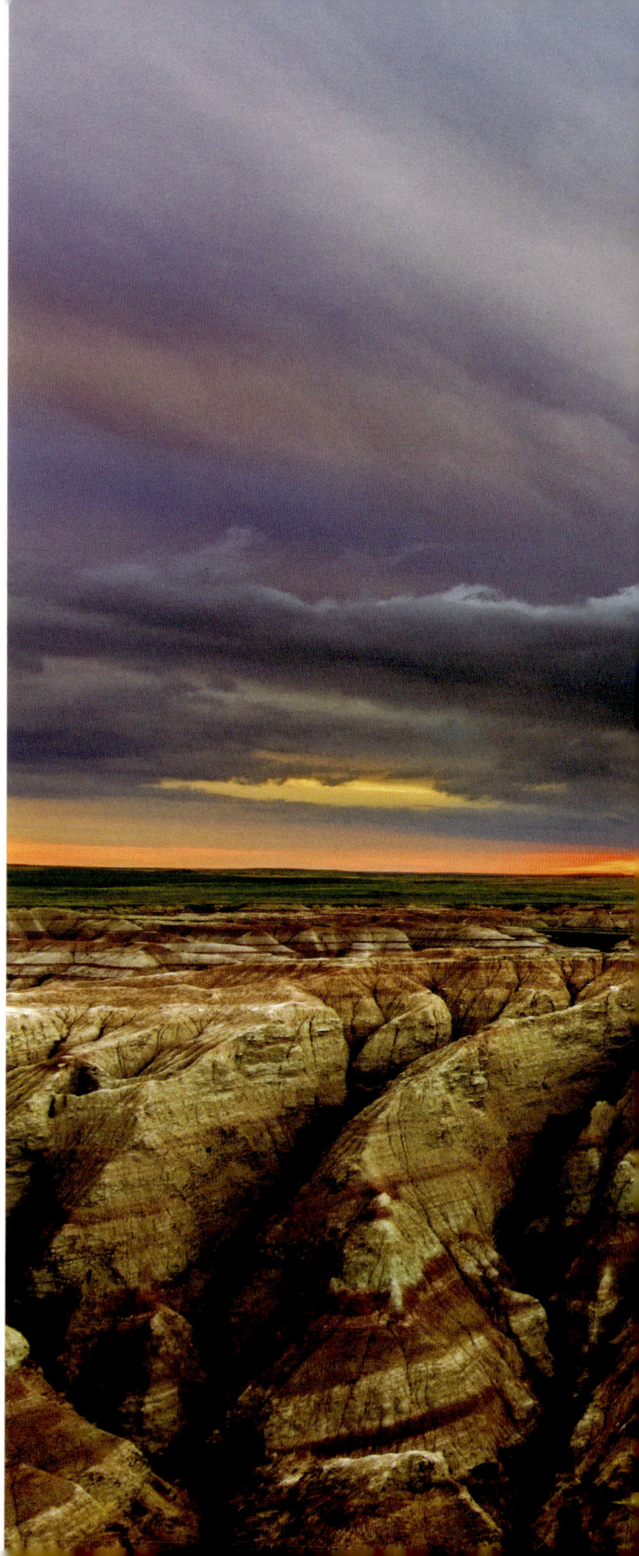

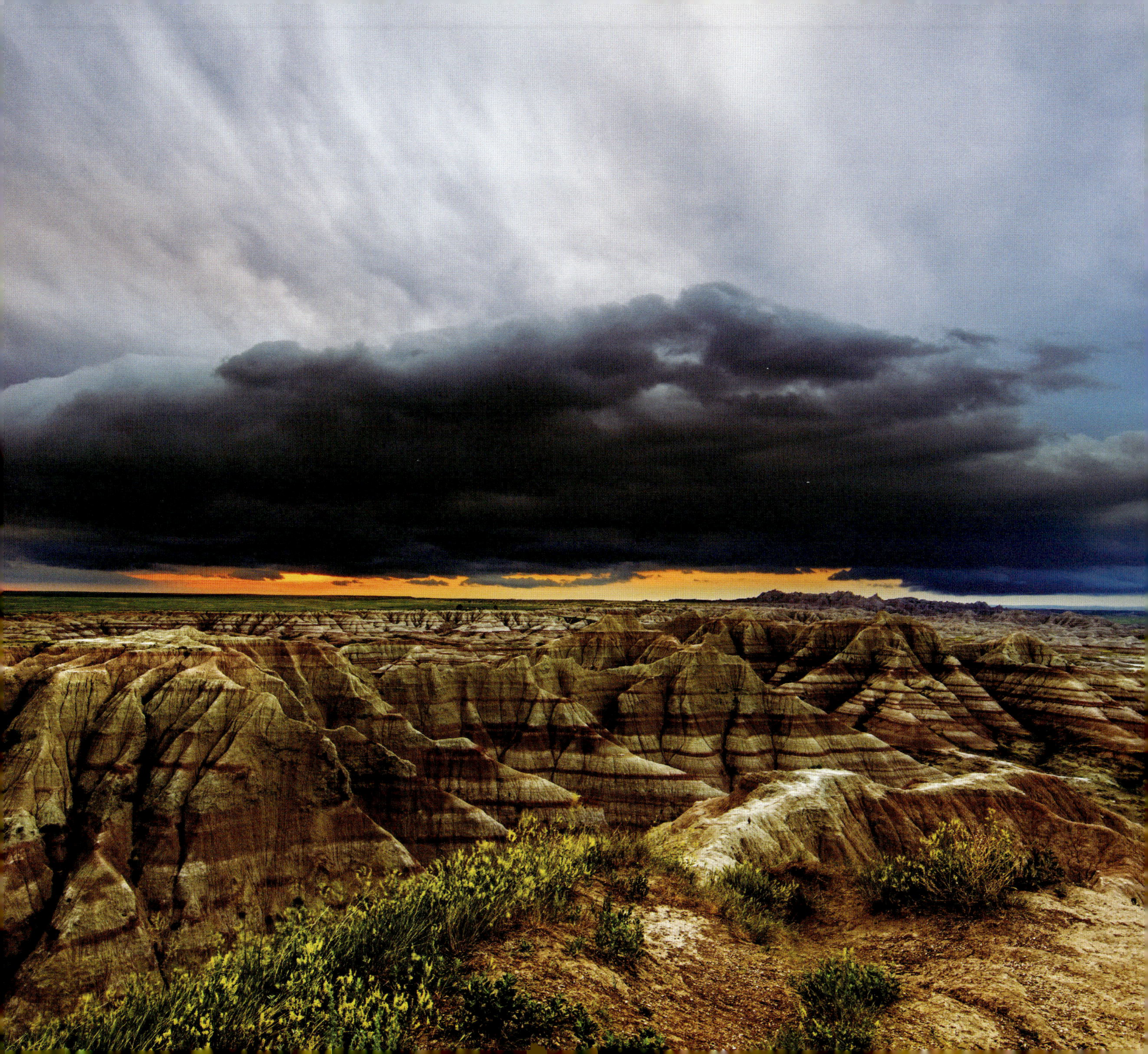

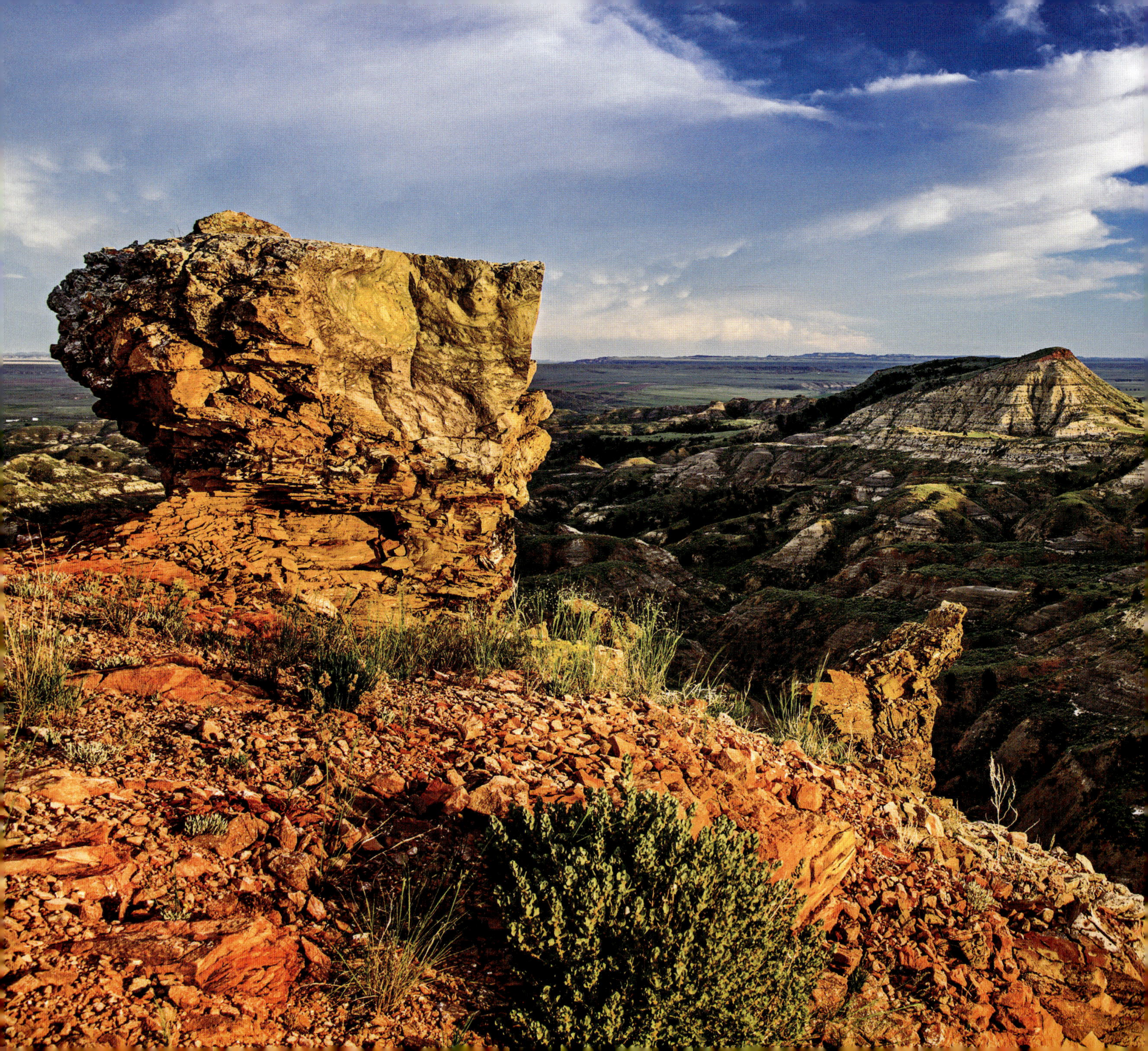

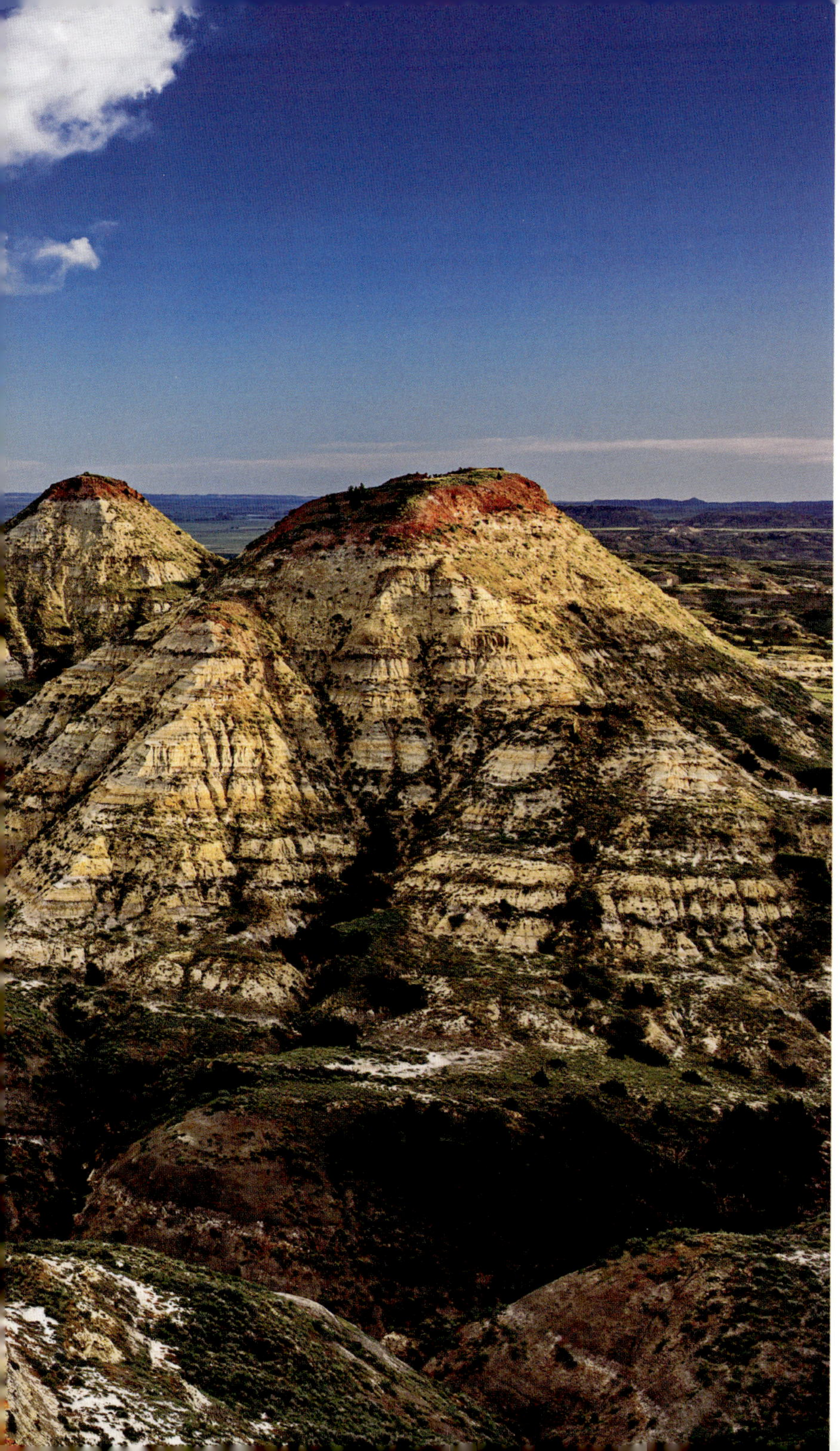

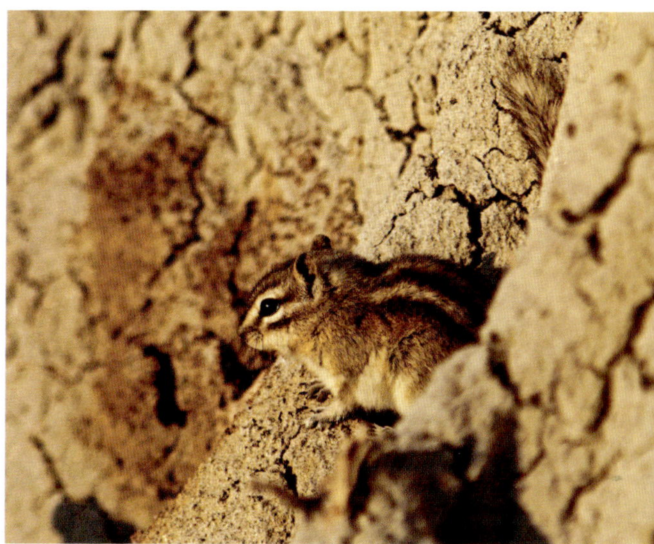

Above: A least chipmunk *(Tamias minimus)* peeks out from a crevice in his badlands home. Found throughout the western United States, this animal is the smallest species of chipmunk and the most widespread in North America.

Left: The badlands formations above the Yellowstone River in Montana's Terry Badlands Wilderness Study Area offer a magical experience in solitude along with biking, hiking, and camping. There are no trails, however, so take a compass.

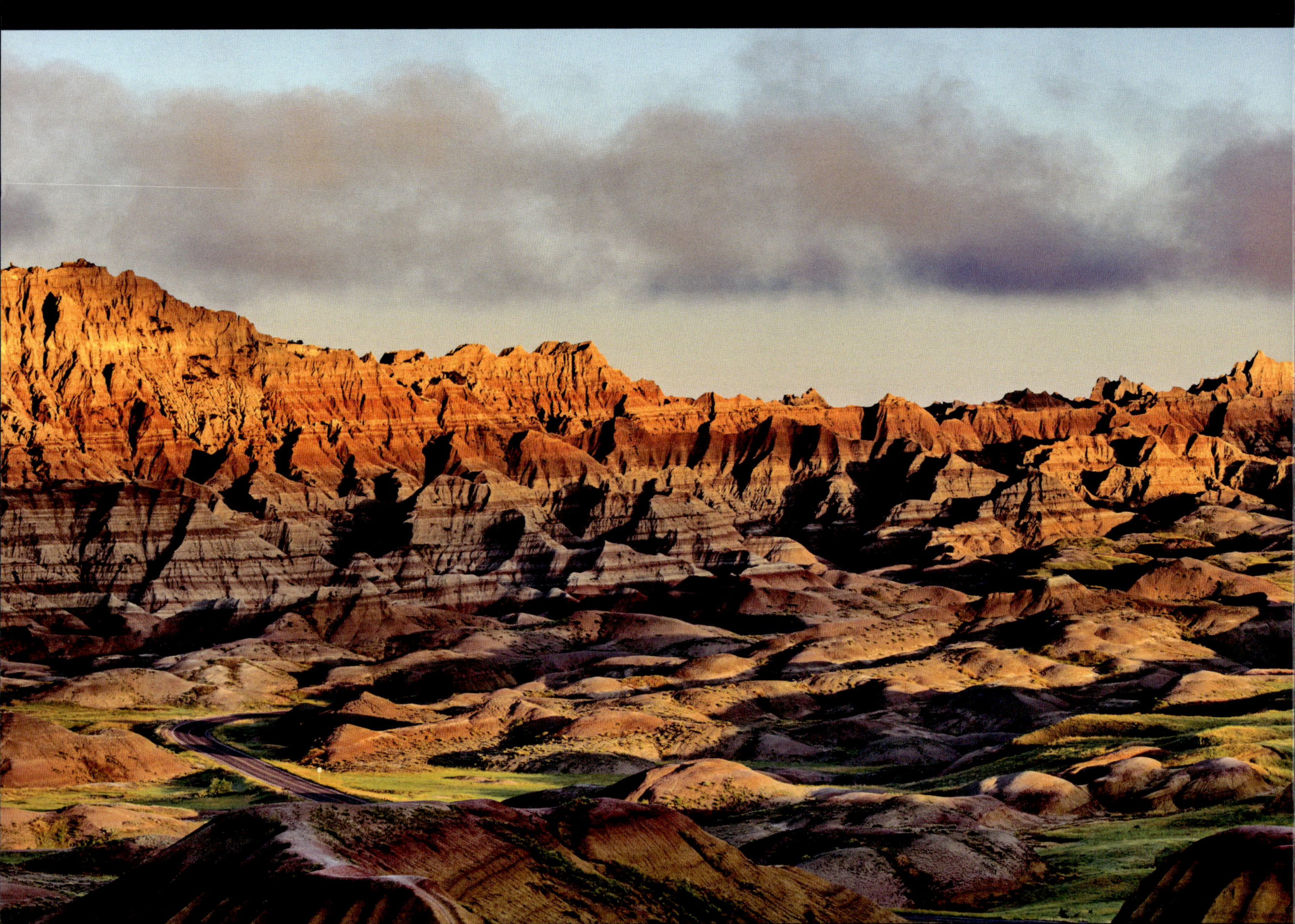

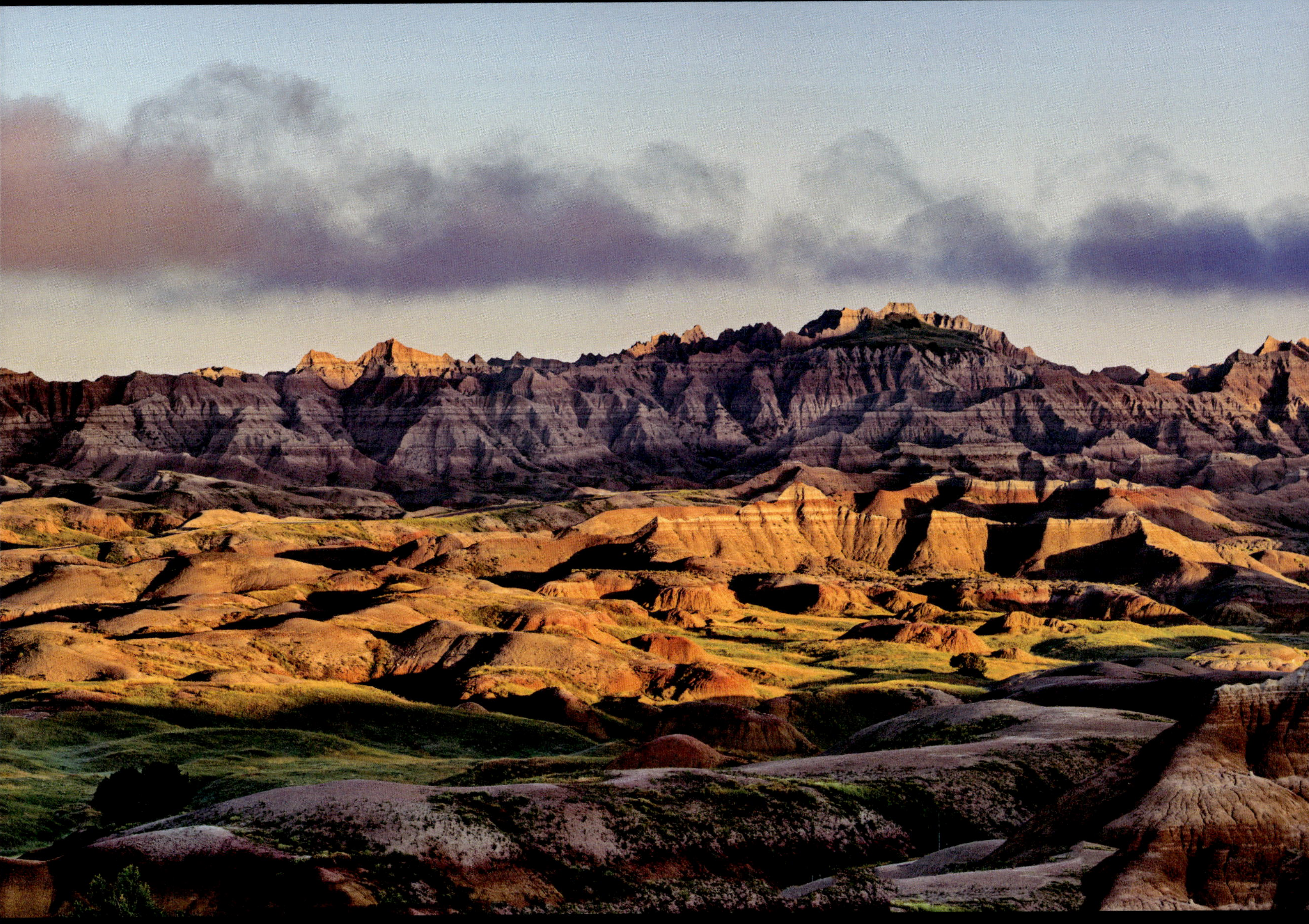

These pinnacles and buttes in Badlands National Park were largely the result of two geologic process: deposition and erosion. Deposition came first about 75 million years ago during the late Cretaceous Period with sedimentary rock layers being deposited, while erosion began about 500,000 years ago when the Cheyenne River captured streams and rivers flowing from the Black Hills.

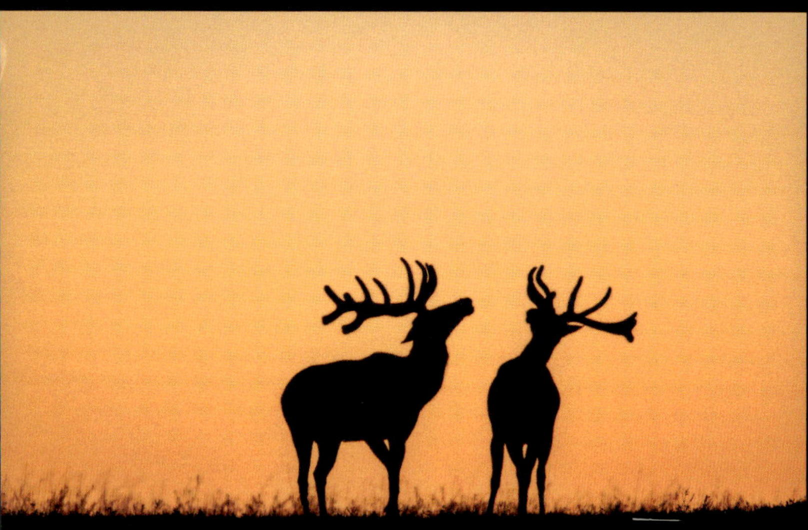

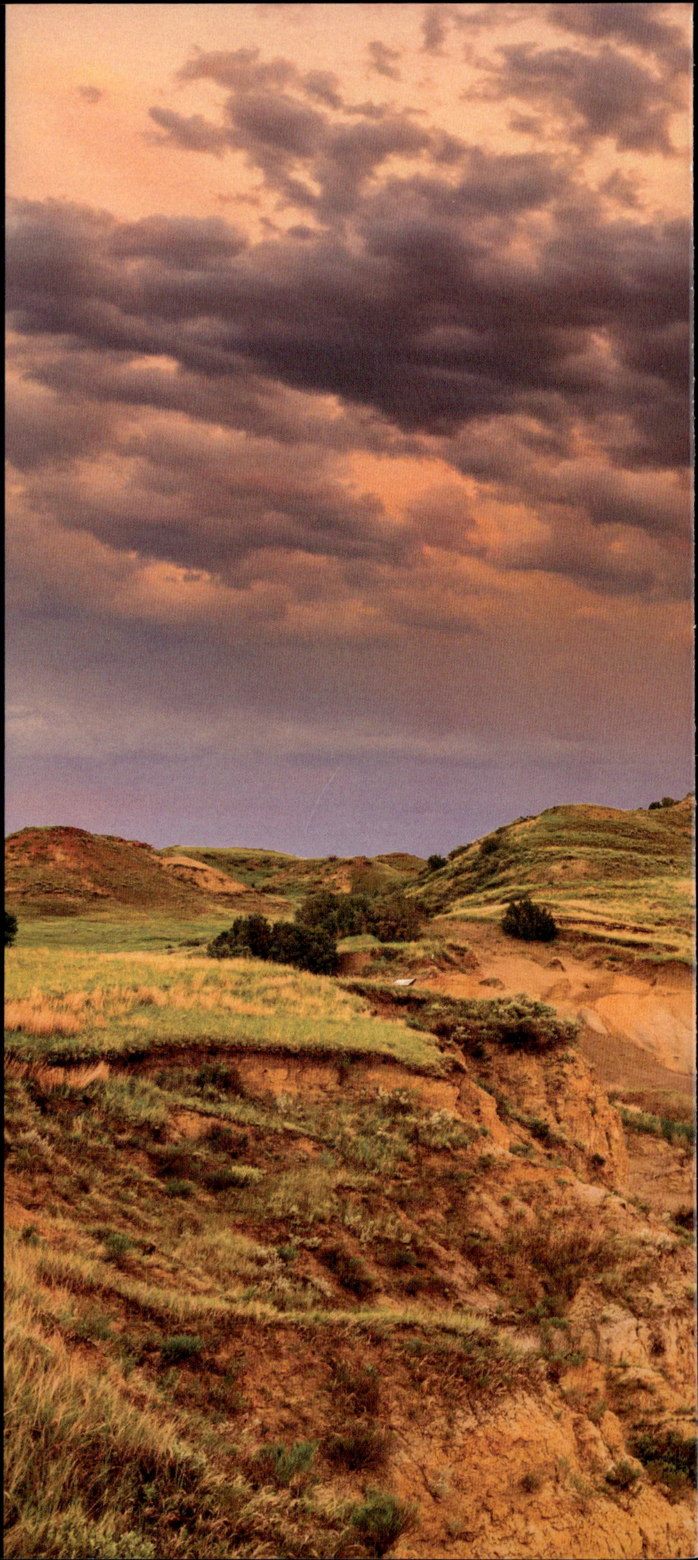

Above: Silhouetted against the sunrise, two bull elk *(Cervus elaphus)* size up each other as the rut gets underway. Though once native to the North Dakota badlands, elk were gone from the region by the late 1800s. Theodore Roosevelt National Park began a reintroduction program in March 1985, bringing in animals from South Dakota's Wind Cave National Park. The park's population currently stands at around 200 and seems very healthy.

Right: A storm gathers and builds over Theodore Roosevelt National Park's Wind Canyon in the South Unit. The Wind Canyon Trail runs alongside this wind-sculpted canyon and offers the best view of the Little Missouri River from the South Unit. Sunsets are great from here, and the trail is an easy hike.

Following page: As he shoots pictures, the shadow of photographer Chuck Haney is cast across colorful sediment layers reflecting Fort Peck Badlands' geologic past.

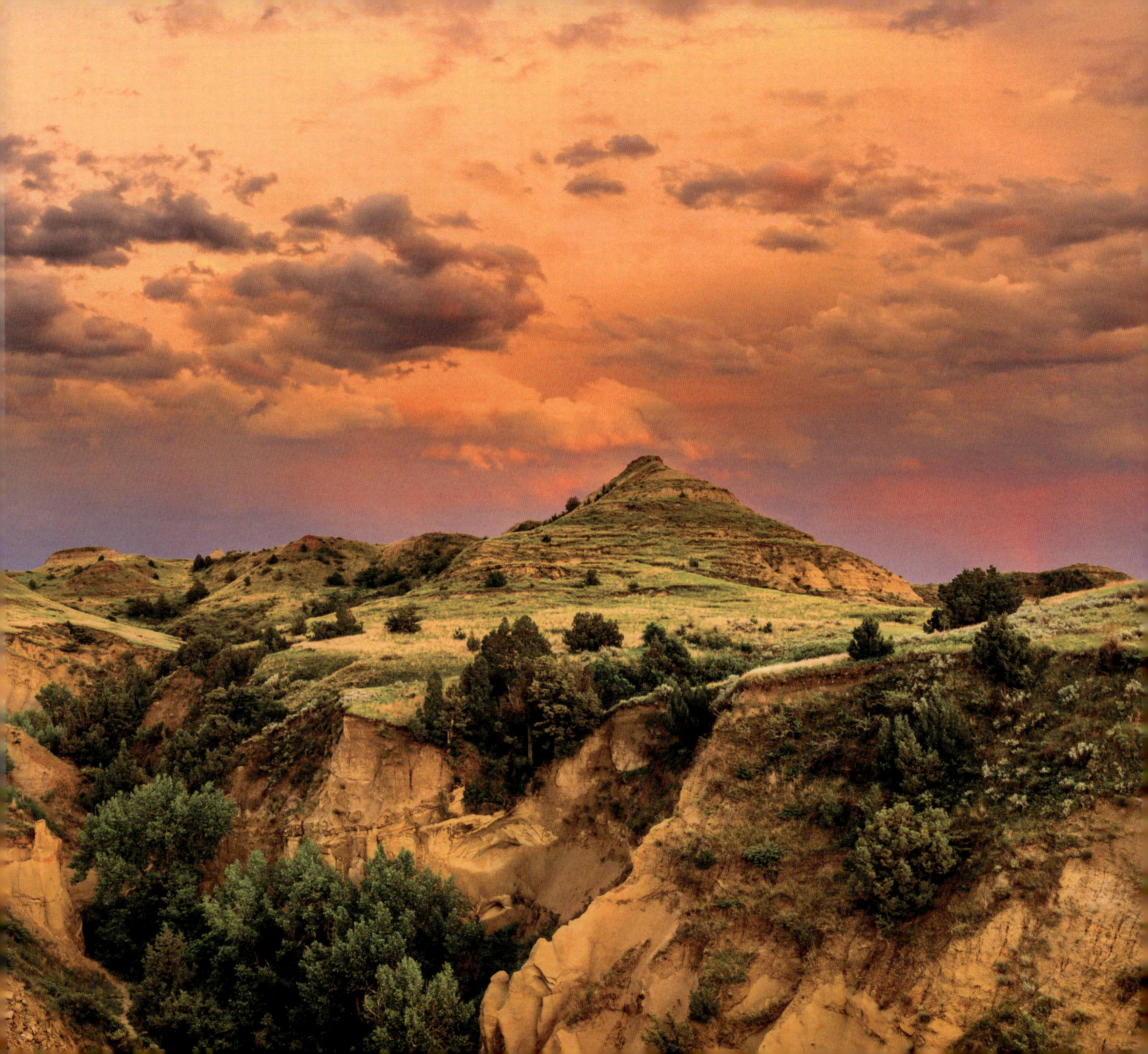

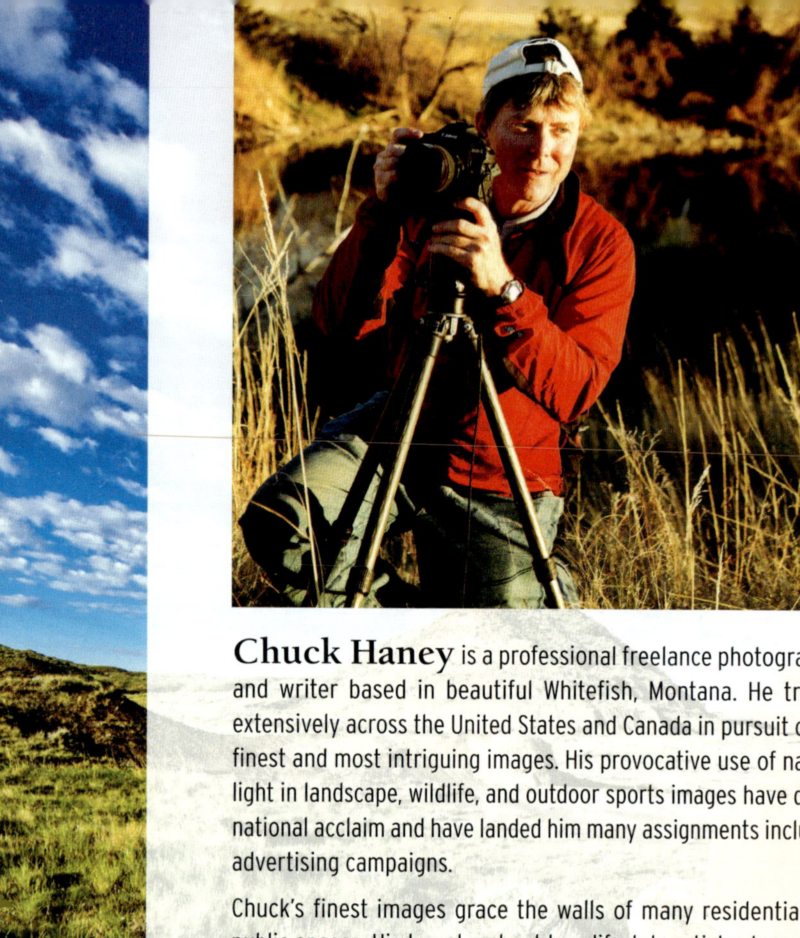

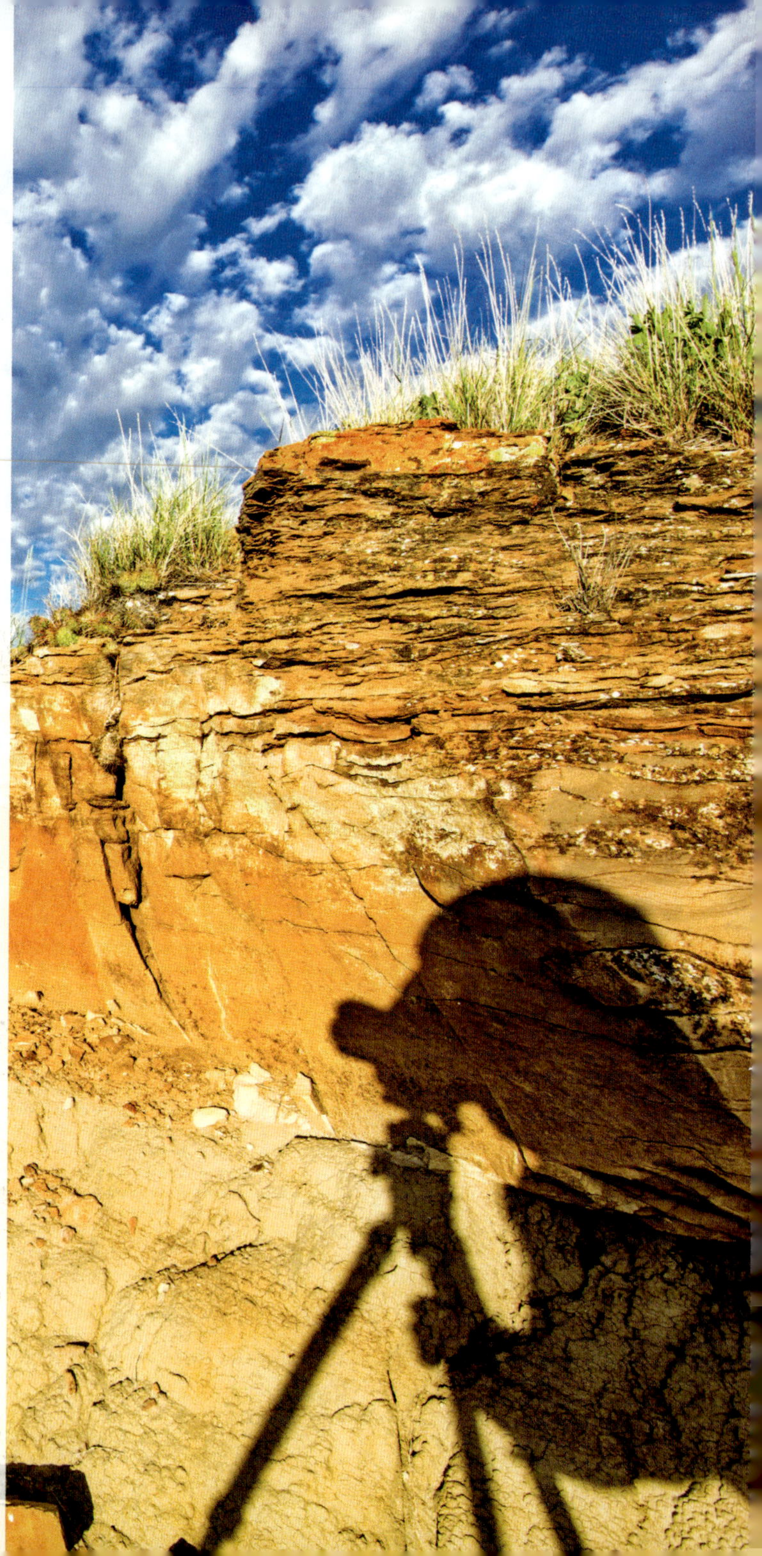

Chuck Haney is a professional freelance photographer and writer based in beautiful Whitefish, Montana. He travels extensively across the United States and Canada in pursuit of the finest and most intriguing images. His provocative use of natural light in landscape, wildlife, and outdoor sports images have drawn national acclaim and have landed him many assignments including advertising campaigns.

Chuck's finest images grace the walls of many residential and public spaces. His travel and outdoor lifestyle articles have been featured in numerous national and regional publications; adding to thirteen coffee-table books, over 190 magazine covers, and sole-photographer calendars to his credit. Chuck enjoys teaching a series of popular photography workshops across the country each year.

To view more of Chuck's photography, please visit his website at www.chuckhaney.com.

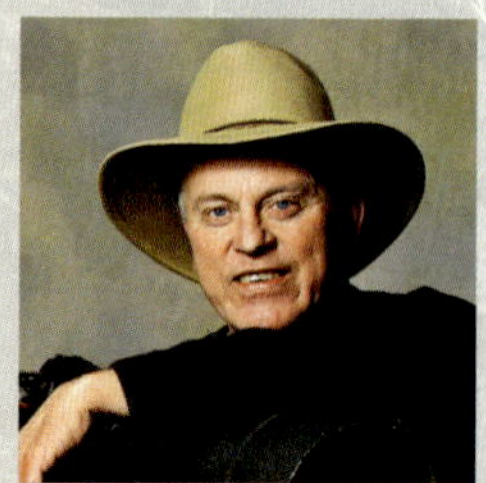

Dick Kettlewell's professional roots are in journalism, having worked for mid and metro-sized daily newspapers for twenty-eight years. During the mid-1990s, he moved to South Dakota's Black Hills in pursuit of a career in outdoor journalism.